WILDLIFE IN NEEDLEPOINT

WILDLIFE IN NEEDLEPOINT

STELLA EDWARDS

ANAYA PUBLISHERS LTD
LONDON

For Andrew, with warmest thanks
for his constant support and encouragement

First published in Great Britain in 1992
by Anaya Publishers Ltd, Strode House,
44–50 Osnaburgh Street, London NW1 3ND

Editors: Gillian Haslam and Eve Harlow
Designer: Clare Clements
Photographer: Lucinda Symons
Artwork: Kate Simunek

The paper in this book has been specifically chosen for its production
from forests which are under sustained yield management.

British Library Cataloguing in Publication Data

Edwards, Stella
Wildlife in Needlepoint
I. Title
746.44

ISBN 1–85470–123–1

Typeset by Servis Filmsetting Ltd, Manchester, England
Colour reproduction by Scantrans Pte Ltd, Singapore
Printed and bound in Singapore by Times Offset Ltd

CONTENTS

The giant panda, symbol of the WWF, is one of the rarest animals in the world. In 1990, only 1000 were known to be living in the wild in China.

FOREWORD

WWF – World Wide Fund for Nature –
is one of the world's leading organisations working to stop,
and eventually reverse, the accelerating degradation
of our planet's natural environment, and to help build a
future in which humans live in harmony with nature.

With almost 5 000 000 regular supporters and a network of 28 national organisations around the world, WWF works to create awareness of threats to nature, to generate and attract, on a worldwide basis, the strongest possible moral, political and financial support for safeguarding the living world, and to convert this support into action based on carefully researched priorities. Since its founding in 1961, WWF – known then as the World Wildlife Fund – has invested more than US$ 300 million in over 5 000 projects in 130 countries.

WWF has a mission with three clear goals: to preserve the variety of life on earth; to help ensure that we use natural resources such as timber, soil, water and fish stocks sustainably, so that they can be renewed for the benefit of future generations; and to encourage the reduction of pollution to a minimum, together with the prevention of wasteful consumption of resources and energy.

By working towards these goals, WWF is also helping people throughout the world to achieve adequate supplies of food and fresh water, security and a decent quality of life, without destroying the natural resource base on which they depend.

WWF's projects, which are undertaken in partnership and cooperation with other conservation groups and institutions and with the support of local communities, are designed to show that conservation of the natural world and sustainable development can be achieved.

Taken together, these factors show WWF is qualified to meet and is actively addressing the challenge to conserve this wonderful living world of ours.

Charles de Haes
Director General WWF – World Wide Fund for Nature

7

INTRODUCTION

The earth's landscapes have changed dramatically during this century with farms becoming even larger, roads cutting through beautiful countryside, more and more housing and factories being built, and the development of new airport sites and marine complexes. Although these are needed, especially in desperately poor countries, there has been little thought as to how they affect the surrounding countryside and the long-term effects on the planet as a whole.

Man has evolved to such a degree that he has forgotten how much he is dependent on the earth. In the developed world food is ready-packaged, clothes are fashion items rather than bought solely for warmth, and heat and light are provided by a flick of a switch. There is no need to worry about these necessities anymore, just about how to pay for them. This leads us to the main problem in the world today – man's greed.

This greed has driven millions of species to extinction. Nowadays, one plant species and 50 animal species are currently being lost *every day*. This is many thousand times the natural rate of extinction. The extinction of species has always been a natural part of evolution with fossil records showing that life originated about 4 billion years ago in the form of bacteria and blue-green algae. For the next 3 billion years evolution was slow but then underwent a surge of diversification during which all the main groups evolved. After this initial mushrooming, the evolution of new species was almost matched by the extinction of old ones with the average duration of a species being about 5 million years. Approximately 90 species became extinct every 100 years and the selective elimination of some species and the advancement of others, including man, has led to the present composition of life on earth.

There are between 5 and 30 million animal and plant species on earth, with around $1\frac{1}{2}$ million having been identified and named. This means that the vast majority of plants and animals facing extinction daily are unknown to science. All animals and plants have a role to play in the working of the natural environment and the extinction of any species could have repercussions throughout the ecosystem. For instance, the rosy periwinkle has been discovered to hold compounds which can cure leukaemia and the pineapple is now known to contain an enzyme which can break down the protein fibrin, which is the major cause of blood clots, leading to heart attacks and strokes. Have other plants been destroyed that could have been vital for our well-being?

RAINFORESTS AND SEAS

The tropical rainforests of the world contain more than half of all the world's species and yet, each year, an area of rainforest the size of Austria is destroyed. Once the trees have gone, the land is used for crops but the top soil soon becomes infertile. As there is nothing to hold it in place the soil is soon washed away. The land is wasted and unfit to use, and so man begins to cut down more forest to use for crops.

The seas are also important and, as yet, have not been fully explored. They contain many geological formations such as deep rift valleys, volcanic mountains and shallow basins with bands or layers of water, each with different controlling currents. Many creatures living in the oceans are still unknown to man – one recent discovery in the Pacific Ocean was a previously unknown species of whale which must have been living for thousands of years. How many others are there?

Man's destruction is affecting the evolution of other animals, but the extent of the damage may not be known for several generations. Creatures are being concentrated into smaller and smaller spaces without our seeming to realise how important *every* creature or plant is for the delicate balance of nature.

The social and hunting way of life of man probably developed about $1\frac{1}{4}$ million years ago and, although he soon learnt to domesticate plants and animals, he retained his hunting knowledge. Today, some races, like the Eskimo, remain hunters but most learned how to grow grain and domesticate livestock. But man began to realise that some animals could be hunted for economical purposes, using their skins for clothing, their blubber for oil, and the bones and tusks for tools and trinkets. Gradually man began to overkill and so upset the balance of nature.

So how can we live in harmony with all other creatures? The answers are there for us to see. In a perfect world there would be plenty of food, warmth and shelter for everyone, and I think that

we who live in the developed world should do more to help those in the Third World who are struggling to survive. Chopping down a tree, or killing a turtle may be a choice between food or starvation. Instead of the exploitation of labour, I think wages should be based on those of western countries. Plants congenial to the local environment should be farmed rather than cleared to make way for plants unnatural to the locality so that pesticides and fertilisers are required on a huge scale. The trade in endangered animals and plants should be seen to be senseless and cease.

SUPPORT FOR THE PLANET

The World Wide Fund for Nature began in 1961 and is the world's leading independent conservation organisation. WWF works to mobilise support for our planet, its ecosystems and wildlife. Its name and panda symbol are known and respected internationally and its reputation had been founded through high profile projects to save species such as the tiger and Arabian oryx. But species cannot be saved unless their habitats are protected and habitats worldwide are facing environmental threats such as ozone depletion, global warming and acid rain. Therefore, WWF campaigns on international issues such as pollution, educating children around the world in environmental responsibility, and tackling problems such as rainforest destruction through high-level lobbying. It is also involved in projects to conserve single species such as elephants, rhinos, giant pandas, gorillas and whales. These kinds of projects conserve entire habitats for the benefit of many other species and also act as catalysts for other sorts of conservation.

WWF is also deeply involved in drawing up international laws and agreements to protect wildlife, including CITES, (the Convention on International Trade in Endangered Species of Wild Fauna and Flora). In 1973 the scale of international trade aroused such concern that a treaty was drawn up in Washington to protect wildlife from over-exploitation and to prevent international trade from threatening species with extinction. So far, over 110 member countries have agreed to ban trade in an agreed list of currently endangered species and to regulate trade in others. The most endangered species covered by this agreement include all apes, the giant panda, great whales, the Asian and African elephants, most of the big cats, all sea turtles and some orchids and cacti.

However, illegal trade still continues and is worth millions of pounds every year.

While I was researching information for this book, I realised that the one common factor the different species have is that their natural habitats are being destroyed. Pollution, overhunting, overfishing and the trade in wildlife all contribute but the major cause is the destruction of wild places to produce land for farming, industry and housing.

Some countries have now realised it makes more commercial sense to keep the natural habitats and ensure that the wildlife is kept alive. The National Game Parks in Africa and India have become increasingly popular places for tourists, generating vast income for these countries. Most of the Great Barrier Reef in Australia is protected and incorporated within a marine park where tourists can swim, dive and fish, under supervision, to ensure that the balance within the park is maintained. In parts of Africa, game wardens, who were once poachers, now not only protect the animals for the tourists, but are also allowed to kill a certain number a year for extra income. As long as there is strict supervision, the rate of decline will subside and the all-important balance between man and animals will be restored.

Scientists are now beginning to realise the immense importance of the contribution of plants to modern industrial processes. Many industries produce toxic or polluting side effects and new techniques to clean up pollution and decontaminate soils are focusing on micro-organisms. Several strains of bacteria, for instance, have been found to be capable of digesting different fractions of oil and cross-breeding has led to a form that will consume 'whole oil'. Jojoba plant seeds produce a yellow, odourless, light liquid wax with properties making it suitable as an engine lubricant, ideal for use in toiletries and cosmetics, and effective as a stabilizer in pharmaceuticals. It seems to be the only vegetable oil currently known which could replace sperm whale oil.

Other properties in nature waiting to be discovered may be greater still. The world is such a complex place and only by ensuring the survival of the raw material, by not destroying forever its natural habitat, can the full potential of the world be realized and its natural wealth not be lost.

In this book, I have included just a small selection of the world's endangered species. I hope their beauty will inspire more people to think long and hard about the very real threat of extinction facing these creatures and plants.

SAFARI

Having travelled to Africa and experienced seeing animals in their natural surroundings, I found it difficult to decide which animals to include in this chapter. So many are endangered – the sleek cheetah and the beautiful leopard – but I felt that the tiger, the lion, the elephant and rhino were synonymous with the landscape, in terms of my designs. The elephants design was inspired by a family group I saw in Kenya, standing under an acacia tree. Seeing the black rhino was a memorable experience, as these are now so rare.

THE ASIAN TIGER

Although few people have seen tigers in the wild, they are among the most familiar animals in the world. Known as the 'Jungle Gentlemen' they are the largest member of the cat family, agile and elegant but at the same time extraordinarily powerful, inspiring both fear and awe.

Today, only four out of the seven species of tiger survive but these still face the threat of extinction. It is not only the uncontrolled shooting, trapping and poisoning of the tiger by man which is reducing its numbers, but also the destruction of the delicately balanced ecosystem where the animal lives. The once vast forests of Asia which teemed with animal life and provided food and shelter are rapidly disappearing to make way for the ever-increasing human population.

The tiger can be found scattered over a large part of Asia, stretching from Turkey in the west to China in the east and ranging from the southern borders of Russia in the north to the Indonesian islands of Java, Sumatra and Bali in the south. However, the tiger is fast disappearing with an estimated total population of 5 000 compared with a figure of 40 000 in India alone in the 1940s. Today, the Indian total stands at 2 000.

Of the seven original varieties of tiger, the Balinese, Caspian and Javanese tigers are now extinct. The Balinese tiger disappeared in the 1940s, the Caspian in the 1970s and the last tracks of the Javanese tiger were seen in 1980.

At the beginning of this century there may have been 100 000 tigers in Asia but now only between 7 000 and 8 000 survive, despite conservation efforts in India, Nepal, Thailand and Indonesia. The four remaining species are the Bengal or Indo-Chinese tiger, the Sumatran tiger, the Chinese tiger and the Siberian tiger.

The Bengal, or Indo-Chinese tiger, is found in Burma, Thailand, Malaysia and Indo-China and is the most numerous although numbers were

*Tigers (*Panthera tigris*) are the largest of all the living cats and are widely distributed, albeit in small numbers, over the Asian continent but mainly found in parts of northern and southern China, India and Sumatra.*

substantially reduced during the Vietnam war when forest areas were depleted and burned by napalm bombing.

The Sumatran tiger is legally protected by the Indonesian government and is found in most of the island's nature reserves. The Chinese tiger, now on the brink of extinction with fewer than 50 thought to exist, is limited to the river forests of the western areas of the Chang Chiang river. The Siberian tiger is the largest of all cats, with about 450 living under legal protection in Siberia and fewer than 50 in north-eastern China.

In 1973 WWF and the Indian government launched *Operation Tiger* with the aim of setting up tiger reserves throughout the country. There were thought to be only about 1 000 Bengal tigers left at that time. There are now 18 reserves in almost all types of tiger habitat and the numbers of Bengal tigers have increased to about 5 000 in India, Nepal and Bangladesh. Elephants, rhinos, swamp deer and wild buffalo are also protected in these reserves. WWF is also working with the Chinese, Thai and Indonesian governments to protect tigers and their habitat.

The tiger is a solitary animal with males and females only meeting in the mating season. Each tiger has a territory which can vary in size from 20–386 square miles (50–1 000 square km) according to the numbers of tigers in the region. They tend to patrol part of their domain at night, covering perhaps 10–20 miles (16–32 km), marking trees and bushes with their scent along the way. The tiger is constantly alert for signs of intruders who will also scent-mark vegetation. Scent-marking is the main challenge over territory and could lead to a fight although the loser will usually retreat rather than fight to the death.

Mating can occur any time through the year with the male and female tigers meeting only for six or seven days. After a gestation period of three months, the female rears the cubs alone.

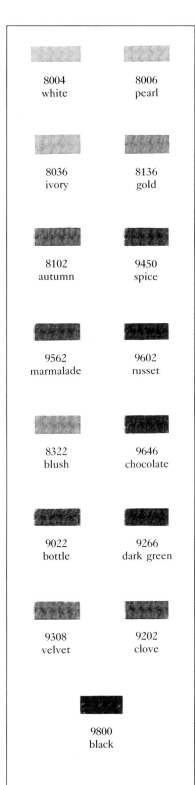

8004 white	8006 pearl
8036 ivory	8136 gold
8102 autumn	9450 spice
9562 marmalade	9602 russet
8322 blush	9646 chocolate
9022 bottle	9266 dark green
9308 velvet	9202 clove
9800 black	

The tiger is a magnificent animal with striking colours which I have tried to capture in this design. To make the tiger as realistic as possible, I worked the fur using single stitches of various shades in places rather than large blocks of colour.

The whiskers were originally a problem but I decided to use a white cross stitch with the top of the cross running in the opposite direction to the rest of the stitches to make them stand out.

MATERIALS
Finished size 15 × 15in (38 × 38cm)
Piece of 10-hole double thread canvas 19 × 19in (48 × 48cm)
Anchor Tapisserie wools: One skein each of 9602 russet, 8036 ivory, 9450 spice, 8004 white
Two skeins each of 8136 gold, 8102 autumn, 8006 pearl
Three skeins each of 9646 chocolate, 9022 bottle
Four skeins of 9562 marmalade
Seven skeins of 9800 black
Small lengths of 9308 velvet, 9202 clove, 9266 dark green for the eyes and 8322 blush for the nose
Piece of backing velvet 17 × 17in (43 × 43cm)
Cushion pad 15 × 15in (38 × 38cm)
Four tassels

PREPARATION
1 Mark the middle of the canvas with vertical and horizontal lines of basting stitches.

WORKING THE EMBROIDERY
2 Begin working the design from the middle of the canvas to ensure the design is central. Follow the key and photograph using half cross stitch throughout.
3 Stitch the tiger's whiskers using a cross stitch with the top of the cross running in the opposite direction to the rest of the design.

FINISHING
4 After completing the embroidery, press the back with a hot steam iron. If the work is misshapen, dampen it with water and pin face downwards on a board, leaving it to dry naturally (see page 105).
5 Trim the unworked canvas to within ½in (12mm) of the embroidery.
6 Place the embroidery and velvet backing together, right sides facing, and stitch on three sides. Insert the cushion pad and close the fourth side with slipstitches. Sew on tassels.

THE RHINOCEROS

The rhinoceros has lived on earth for over 50 million years. It is a massive, powerful and imposing creature, yet totally vulnerable to the whims of mankind.

There are five different species of rhinoceros: the white, black, Indian, Sumatran and Javan. Although descended from a common ancestor, they differ widely in appearance, size and behaviour. None of the species is numerous although there are more of the two African species (the whites and blacks) at present than the rarer Asian varieties.

The illegal trade in rhino horn has been the main cause of decreasing numbers of black rhinoceros (Diseros bicornis) with only some 3 500 left today in Africa.

The white rhinoceros is the most numerous with numbers in excess of 4 600. The population has not always been so healthy, however, and were it not for the actions of a handful of dedicated conservationists a century ago, the white rhino species would have died out.

Due to unprecedented poaching during the past two decades, the numbers of black rhino have plummeted from an estimated 65 000 in 1970 to fewer than 3 500 today. In Kenya alone, despite a total ban on all hunting, the population has dropped from 20 000 to about 200.

The great one-horned, or Indian, rhino is the most prehistoric-looking of all the rhino with its heavily folded skin resembling armour-plating. This animal is well protected in both India and Nepal where its current population of some 2 000 is increasing at more than five per cent a year, a factor influenced both by good protection and the lack of organised poaching.

The Javan, or lesser one-horned Asian, rhino is smaller than the Indian rhino although similar in appearance. During the last century Javan rhino were so numerous and considered to be such pests that a bounty was offered for their deaths which led to the rhinos being hunted almost to extinction. For many years WWF has been supporting the Ujung Kulon National Park in Java where the rhinos have increased from 25 in 1967 to over 50 today, although poaching is still a problem. WWF is also talking with the government in Vietnam to

establish a protected area for the few rhinos still surviving there, estimated at between 8 and 15 animals.

The Asian two-horned, or Sumatran, rhino is the smallest of the species and was widely distributed throughout Indonesia at the turn of the century. Its decline can be attributed to hunting as well as loss of habitat due to forest clearance. There are only 400 to 900 Sumatran rhinos today.

Hunters have killed rhinos for thousands of years in their quest for its valued horn which has been used by some cultures as a mystical drug. Many orientals who use western drugs such as aspirin and antibiotics, still believe in the curative powers of powdered rhino horn for colds and fever, headaches, arthritis and lumbago and it is commonly prescribed alongside, or as an alternative to, modern, scientifically-based drugs.

As well as trying to close the illegal trade markets in rhino horn, WWF is experimenting with substitute materials, such as water buffalo horn, which could be acceptable in eastern pharmaceuticals.

The crack-down on illegal trading in rhino horn has not, unfortunately, deterred either the poachers or the dealers and users. In Kenya today there are specialist rhino patrols that monitor and stay with the rhinos every day from daybreak to sunset. In the recent past, corrupt park rangers could easily kill a rhino and sell the horn but now the rangers are well paid to protect the animals. The sentences for convicted poachers are severe and the rangers have authority to kill poachers if necessary.

Rhinos are solitary creatures, apart from the mothers and their calves. The male and females have no fixed breeding season and after mating they part leaving the mother to raise the calf. A single calf is born after a gestation period of 15 months and suckles until it is well over a year old. The young rhinoceros will stay with its mother for the next 3 to 5 years until the next calf is born.

| 9656 | 9658 | 9642 | 9314 | 9002 | 9006 |
| pepper | smoke | chutney | hawthorn | apple | green |

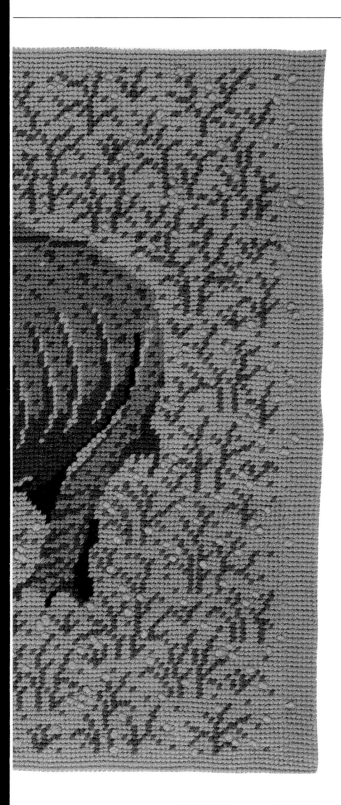

| 8232 | 9800 |
| apricot | black |

I felt I had to include the rhinoceros in this book because it is so endangered and I feel very strongly about these animals since watching a group of three rhinos in the wild. One was the mother accompanied by a male calf aged about four years and a baby about a month old. It was a encouraging sight as it proves the conservation programme in Kenya is beginning to work.

I chose to the black rhino as the inspiration for a footstool design, adding a soft green background with darker sprigs of green grass and small knots to represent delicate peach flowers. In the wild, rhinos seem to have a hide of many colours, usually in shades of dark red brown or yellowy green brown. They love to bathe in mud to prevent their skin from dying out and, depending on their habitat, this mud can be either a rich ochre or a yellowy green.

MATERIALS
Finished size: 16 × 12in (40 × 30cm)
Piece of 12-hole canvas 19 × 15in (48 × 38cm)
Anchor Tapisserie wools:
One skein each of 9800 black, 9642 chutney,
* 9656 pepper, 9314 hawthorn*
Two skeins of 8232 apricot
Three skeins of 9658 smoke
Four skeins of 9006 green
Eleven skeins of 9002 apple
Rectangular footstool 16 × 12in (40 × 30cm)

PREPARATION
1 Mark the middle of the canvas with vertical and horizontal lines of basting stitches.

WORKING THE EMBROIDERY
2 Begin working the design from the middle of the canvas to ensure the design is central. Follow the key and photograph using half cross stitch, leaving the peach flowers to last.
3 Using the apricot wool, work knots over the background, scattering them in groups.

FINISHING
4 If the finished embroidery is misshapen, dampen it and stretch it back to shape by pinning it face downwards on a board covered with a cloth. Leave it to dry naturally (see page 105).
5 Trim the unworked canvas to within 1in (2.5cm) of the embroidery.
6 Attach the embroidery to the footstool pad and cover the underside of the stool with fabric (see page 106).

THE AFRICAN ELEPHANT

The elephant is the largest of all land mammals and has existed for some 5 million years. Today there are just two species, the African elephant and the Asian elephant, the sole survivors of more than 300 species of trunked animals, some of which were far larger than the elephants of today and roamed in Europe, North and South America as well as in Africa and India.

The differences in African and Asian elephants are mainly in body shape and size, notably their different size of ears. It is said that the African elephant has an ear the shape of Africa and the Asian the shape of India. Classed in different generic groups which denotes differences in their skeletons, the two creatures live very similar lives.

Elephants are unique in that they have both tusks and trunks. It seems that the trunk evolved to enable the elephant to reach the ground as its head had become so big to support its tusks.

The trunk is very adaptable. It is mainly used for breathing but can also test the air for scent, act as a hose for drinking and showering (both liquids and dust), sound as a trumpet and be used as a highly flexible working tool. The trunk can break off branches and hoist huge logs, and be used as an expressive organ of affection to greet and caress fellow elephants.

Tusks are simply enlarged incisor teeth in the upper jaw with a quarter of their length lying within the socket, held by a mass of tough fibrous tissue. They continue to grow throughout an elephant's life, so big tusks denote relatively old elephants. The tusks are mainly used as tools rather than as weapons for prising bark away from tree trunks and for digging. The male and female elephants in Africa usually have tusks but in Asia only some males bear tusks, the percentage of which varies in different regions.

Elephants are one of the few species that live together in family groups. Usually the females stay together throughout their lives with the males living alone or with various different groups. The

The African elephant (Loxodonta africana) *is one of a few species that stay together in family groups. Hunted for ivory, elephant numbers have dropped from literally millions a hundred years ago to 625 000 in 1989.*

———— • ————

females are ruled by a matriarch, aged about 50 or 60, who is usually the largest of the group as elephants continue to grow throughout their lives. Through experience she knows when and where the trees are coming into fruit, where the grass is lush and where there is water to drink and leads the herd along traditional routes that have been trodden by many elephant generations.

Females can breed between the ages ten and eighteen until they reach 50. However, this depends on the right conditions prevailing, such as the amount of food available, the stress caused by harassment by poachers and lack of land space due to human settlement. One calf is born after a 22 month gestation period and is looked after by all the females in the herd.

Both Asian and African elephants are now endangered species, not only because of their ivory but also because of the amount of land they need to feed on. Elephants spend most of their lives grazing and browsing in order to maintain their enormous bodies and therefore require a large area of land to survive. It is estimated that around 500 elephants require between 190–1 900 square miles (500–5 000 square kilometres) depending on the amount of food available. No area of this size can be left solely for elephants so it is imperative that man works together with the animals.

Demand for ivory started during the early years of the first century AD and peaked in 1914 with 1 000 tonnes leaving Africa annually, probably resulting in 50 000 elephant deaths a year. However, by the 1920's ivory had become less fashionable except for items such as billiard balls and knife handles.

Unfortunately the demand for ivory has grown again leading to the widespread killing of elephants. After pressure from conservationists, including WWF, a worldwide ban on the ivory trade was instigated in 1990 and there are indications that the ban is working.

8006 pearl	9442 magnolia
9524 treacle	9448 bronze
9526 amber	9450 spice
9624 brick	9564 chestnut
9646 chocolate	9684 mahogany
9800 black	9372 putty
9656 pepper	9658 smoke
9014 spruce	9016 forest
8686 bluebell	9020 moss

This group of elephants is becoming a more common sight in eastern Africa and I was fortunate enough to see this particular herd in Kenya recently and interpreted them into this realistic needlepoint design. The elephants are standing under an acacia tree with the nest of small weaver birds hanging from the branches.

MATERIALS
Finished size 20 × 19½in (50 × 49cm)
Piece of 10-hole double thread canvas size 24 × 24in (61 × 61cm)
Separate piece size 14 × 7in (35 × 18cm) for tags
Anchor Tapisserie wools:
One skein each of 9684 mahogany, 9656 pepper, 8006 pearl, 9800 black, 9524 treacle, 9526 amber, 9016 forest, 9014 spruce
Two skeins each of 9646 chocolate, 9564 chestnut, 9624 brick, 9020 moss
Three skeins each of 9372 putty, 9450 spice, 9448 bronze
Seven skeins each of 9658 smoke, 8686 bluebell
13 skeins of 9442 magnolia
Piece of backing fabric 22 × 22in (56 × 56cm)
Four smaller pieces each 2 × 4in (5 × 10cm)
Pole and brackets to hang the design on the wall

PREPARATION
1 Mark the middle of the canvas with vertical and horizontal lines of basting stitches.

WORKING THE EMBROIDERY
2 Begin working the design from the middle of the canvas. Follow the key and photograph, using half cross stitch throughout.
3 Using the smaller piece of canvas, embroider the four tags for hangers.

FINISHING
4 Stretch the canvas by dampening it and pinning it to a board covered with a cloth, leaving it to dry naturally (see page 105).
5 Back the four tags with fabric, fold in half and carefully attach to the wallhanging.
6 With right sides together, sew the backing fabric to three sides of the embroidery, leaving the top open.
7 Trim the excess canvas, cutting the corners diagonally and turn right sides out.
8 Slipstitch the lining to the embroidery at the top, ensuring the ends of the tags are covered.
9 Fold and sew the tag ends over the pole to support the hanging.

THE AFRICAN LION

The lion is known as the 'king of the beasts' and has been the symbol of strength and majesty since the beginning of recorded history. The male lion is an impressive creature with its huge size, voluminous mane and powerful build and has the respect of both man and other animals.

For centuries it was considered an act of courage to kill a lion. In 1370 BC the Egyptian pharoah Amenhotep II hunted lions to show his prowess, and until recently the Masai people of East Africa used to spear lions to prove their manhood. However, the lion has almost disappeared due to man's hunting. Lions had vanished from Greece by AD 100 and from most of Asia by the mid-twentieth century. In India there are now just a few hundred lions in the small Gir sanctuary in the state of Gujarat.

At one time Africa was home to ten different breeds of lions. The Berber lion of North Africa became extinct by the 1920s due to man's continual hunting. South of the Sahara, lions have been shot or poisoned into extinction by cattle ranchers as the animals posed a serious threat to the herds. Cape lions of South Africa were also affected by the new settlers and have been extinct for over 100 years.

Today in Africa lions are only found in the savanna regions, mainly in the east, where enlightened game policies of various governments protects the species. The best area is the Serengeti where, in 1929, about 900 square miles were made into a game reserve, preserving a good population of the Masai lion. In 1940 the area was increased to 5 000 square miles and became a national park. Here, and in many other smaller game reserves, the lions live a relatively natural life which is helping to protect the species.

Lion society is complex and not a rigidly defined social group. Each pride has between two and 15 lionesses plus their cubs, and between one and four adult males (often brothers) who are not always permanent pride members. The females

*Today, the lion (*Panthera leo*) is protected by the enlightened game policies of several African governments and now lives a fairly natural life in special game reserves.*

are all related and usually remain together for life whereas the males stay with the pride from six months to six years.

Generally, it is the lionesses who hunt for food for the whole pride while the males rest in the sun or under a shady tree. The lioness is not the fastest of animals, and certainly not the surest hunter, often seeming clumsy, noisy and sometimes too heavy. In contrast, a cheetah or leopard moves swiftly and sleekly close to the ground and will usually bring down its intended victim every time. A lioness, on the other hand, may lunge 20 times a day before managing to catch one good feed for the pride.

If a male lion decides to hunt there are few animals that can, or will, stand against him. His sheer strength means that one paw swipe can break the neck of a zebra, and when stalking he can terrorize his intended victim into near paralysis merely by making his intention to kill clear. Climbing can be no defense against a charging lion since his agility matches his power. Male lions have been seen to jump as high as 12 to 36ft (3·5–11m) and they often climb trees.

When a lioness becomes pregnant she will continue to hunt for as long as she can. Just before giving birth she seeks out a suitable cave as near to water as possible where she can give birth to as many as six cubs. When the cubs are 5 months old, they are ready to learn how to hunt and at 15 months they are able to capture their own prey. At 18 months the mother ceases to care for the cubs as she will soon have another litter.

The noises made by lions are really signals. When a male roars with throat and chest at 'full throttle' he is merely making a statement of territorial possession. When on the move, he grunts to keep his path clear of smaller animals. When prowling for food he roars in a relatively restrained way, when angry he growls but when he starts to cough it means he is genuinely upset and about the charge!

The lion is an awesome animal and, although he can be frightening, I have tried to concentrate on his strength and majesty. The design is intricate, using single stitches of several colours among the main colours which help to give movement and make the animal come alive.

When studying lions for this design I was surprised at the amount of grey colour found in their coats. Before seeing the animals in their natural African habitat, I presumed they would be full of rich golds, yellow and browns but the colouring is actually much softer. I have used these softer tones to make a border and have added tassels to each corner to complete the design.

MATERIALS
Cushion size 15 × 15in (38 × 38cm)
Piece of 10-hole double thread canvas 19 × 19in (48 × 48cm)
Anchor Tapisserie wools:
One skein each of 9800 black, 8036 ivory, 9656 pepper
Two skeins of 9524 treacle
Three skeins of 8264 auburn
Four skeins of 8054 maize
Five skeins each of 9642 chutney, 9450 spice
Six skeins of 9492 beige
Small lengths of 8322 blush, 8006 pearl, 9308 velvet, 9312 turmeric
Piece of backing velvet 17 × 17in (43 × 43cm)
Cushion pad 15 × 15in (38 × 38cm)
Four tassels

PREPARATION
1 Mark the middle of the canvas with horizontal and vertical lines of basting stitches.

WORKING THE EMBROIDERY
2 Following the key and photograph, start stitching from the middle of the canvas and use half cross stitch throughout.

FINISHING
3 Press the embroidery on the back with a hot steam iron and gently ease it into shape. If it is misshapen dampen the embroidery and pin it to a fabric-covered board, leaving it to dry naturally.
4 Stitch the backing fabric to the embroidery, right sides facing, on three sides only.
5 Trim the canvas to within ½in (12mm) of the embroidery. Turn right sides out, stuff with a cushion pad and sew the open seam using slip-stitch. Sew small tassels to each corner if desired.

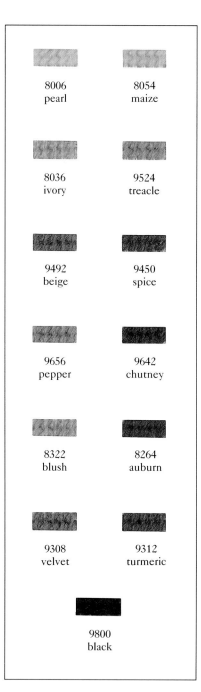

8006 pearl	8054 maize
8036 ivory	9524 treacle
9492 beige	9450 spice
9656 pepper	9642 chutney
8322 blush	8264 auburn
9308 velvet	9312 turmeric
9800 black	

TROPICAL RAINFORESTS

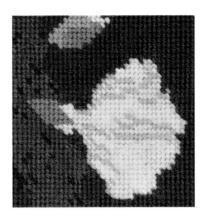

I tried to make the designs for this chapter very different from each other, from the panda eating bamboo and the Queen Alexandra's birdwing butterfly to the bright macaws and the delicate rosy periwinkle. All the designs were fascinating to embroider, perhaps especially the macaws, which did not really come to life until the creamy background was stitched, which made the vivid reds, oranges and blues stand out against the lush vegetation.

THE GIANT PANDA

The giant panda is one of the rarest animals in the world. In 1990 there were only about 1 000 living wild in China and 15 living in zoos outside China. His strong appeal to human beings is not so much due to his rarity, but his teddy-bear appearance, enhanced by striking coat markings (especially the large patches around the eyes), his solitary lifestyle, rolling gait and apparent preference for taking a nap rather than physical exertion. The panda is not cuddly, however, as his fur is rather coarse and greasy. He is a very powerful creature with a strong grip, claws and a formidable bite.

*One of the rarest animals in the world, the giant panda (*Ailuropoda melanoleuca*) is found in the bamboo forests of south-west China.*

Although giant pandas have lived in China for thousands of years and were highly valued by the ancient Chinese emperors, there have never been many of them. They were only discovered by the West when a French priest, Father Armand David, saw the animal while visiting China in 1869 and brought its skin and bones back to Paris to be studied by scientists. The first living pandas were taken to the USA in 1936.

Giant pandas can be found in the cool, damp and misty bamboo forests high up in the mountains of Sichuan, in south-west China. The bamboo grows in tightly-packed thickets, virtually impenetrable by man, which provides the panda's main source of food. Although originally carnivores, pandas have developed a vegetarian diet due to the abundance of bamboo and the lack of competition from other animals to eat it. Pandas have specially adapted paws with which they are able to grip the bamboo. A unique 'thumb' has developed which is a specially enlarged wrist bone covered by a leathery pad.

The panda only absorbs 10 per cent of the nutritional value of the food he eats. This means that the animal has to eat a lot and process the food through the body quickly to make room for more. Pandas can eat for 8 hours at a time, then sleep for 4 hours or so, only to wake up and begin eating again. This continues through the day and night, and if not supplemented by the occasional cane rat or some fish, the panda's diet is near to starvation.

The bamboo plants, which make 99 per cent of the panda's diet, are unpredictable in growth. For up to a 100 years a particular species grows by spreading long, underground branches and sending up shoots which feed the panda. The shoots then suddenly flower, produce seeds and die. Many pandas die of starvation if several bamboo species do this at the same time.

Pandas can mate and have young when they are about 6 years old. During spring the normally solitary animals seek each other out by scent, mate and then return to their own territories. Five months later one or two panda cubs are born which begin to crawl at about 3 months old and are able to look after themselves at 6 months, becoming fully grown at 4 years. Their average lifespan is 12 years.

Giant pandas have become increasingly rare due to several factors. In recent years there have been several flowerings of bamboo resulting in many panda deaths and, due to the animals' slow reproductive cycle, it takes a few years to replace those which have died. The bamboo is also being destroyed by people who need the land for farms and villages. Hunting is another factor which still continues even though it has been banned by the Chinese government.

However, panda reserves have been set up to protect both the panda and its bamboo. The largest reserve was created in 1975 at Wolong in China and, in 1980, in a joint project between the Chinese government and WWF, a special panda-breeding and research centre was built there. There are also educational programmes for the local villages, teaching them about the need to protect pandas and why they are so special. Nowadays if a panda does cause damage to the farm crops, locals are compensated.

8006
pearl

9800
black

9156
jade

Giant pandas look so appealing that I could not resist making these coordinating items which are both very quick to make.

The pincushion shows the symbol of the World Wild Fund for Nature, using the black, white and green colours that are so well-known with a black and white chequer-board effect on the back. This pincushion is very simple and is an ideal project for a child to start with. The edges have been joined together using long armed cross stitch to give a neat finish but an over stitch or slipstitch will work just as well. Long armed cross stitch and slipstitch are both described on page 104.

The purse also uses a panda motif but this time I have made him more realistic, seating him munching bamboo in the forest. Here the panda and background are stitched using half cross stitch with the bamboo and leaves created by catching short stitches into the main embroidery. More leaves can be added to the design if you wish or different shades of green can be used. To make the leaves and bamboo stems appear so delicate I have split the wool yarn, just using two of the strands which make up a complete yarn. This is not difficult to do although only short lengths of 12in (30cm) should be used. For a variation in texture you may like to try introducing a few stitches in stranded embroidery cotton.

PINCUSHION MATERIALS
Finished size 4 × 4in (10 × 10cm)
Two pieces of 12-hole interlock canvas, size 6 × 6in (15 × 15cm)
Anchor Tapisserie wools:
Two skeins each of 9156 jade, 9800 black and 8006 pearl
Toy stuffing

PREPARATION
1 Mark the middle of both pieces of canvas with horizontal and vertical lines of basting stitches.

WORKING THE EMBROIDERY
2 Begin working the design from the middle of the canvas, working outwards and using half cross stitch throughout and following the colours of the key and photograph. Finish by working the rows of green. Work the back in the same way.

FINISHING
3 Press the back of the embroidery using a hot steam iron, gently pulling it back into the shape (see page 105).
4 Trim the unworked canvas back to about ½in (12mm) from the edges of the embroidery, cutting the corners diagonally. This helps to make sharper corners when you fold the edges under.

5 Fold the unworked canvas to the wrong side of the embroidery.

6 With wrong sides together, sew the two sides of the pincushion together with long armed cross stitch starting 1in (2.5cm) before one corner, sewing all the way around three sides but leaving a 1½in (4cm) gap.

7 Stuff the pin cushion with the toy stuffing and close the gap with the long armed cross stitch.

PANDA PURSE MATERIALS
Finished size 4¾ × 4in (12 × 10cm)
Piece of 12-hole interlock canvas, size 15 × 7in
 (38 × 18cm)
Anchor Tapisserie wools:
One skein of 8992 grass
Five skeins of 9442 magnolia
Short lengths of 9640 nutmeg, 9018 leaf, 9800 black,
 8006 pearl
Piece of backing fabric 14 × 6in (36 × 15cm)
Press fastener

PREPARATION

1 Mark the centre of the canvas with horizontal and vertical lines of basting stitches.

WORKING THE EMBROIDERY

2 Stitch the panda, background and outside row of green in half cross stich, following the key and photograph.

3 Using short lengths of nutmeg, leaf green and grass green divided into 2 strands, work stitches to create the effects of bamboo and leaves.

FINISHING

4 Press the embroidery on the back with a hot steam iron, gently pulling it back into shape (see page 105).

5 Trim the unworked canvas to within ½in (12mm) of the embroidery, cutting the corners diagonally.

6 Fold the unworked canvas to the wrong side of the embroidery.

7 With wrong sides facing, slipstitch the lining fabric to the embroidery ensuring no unworked canvas shows.

8 Fold one third of the embroidery over (the plain section) and catch it to the back of the purse with long armed cross stitch, or over stitch.

9 Sew the ball part of a press fastener to the bottom of the flap and the other part to the bag to correspond. Alternatively, small squares of Velcro can be used.

8006 pearl	9800 black	9442 magnolia
9640 nutmeg	9018 leaf	8992 grass

TROPICAL BUTTERFLIES

The butterfly's range, diversity and brilliance of colour is unrivalled anywhere, except possibly by the birds. Butterflies have achieved an almost worldwide distribution though, as with most animal groups, there is a greater diversity to be found in the tropics.

The butterfly life cycle is no less remarkable than the beauty of the adult. The transformation or metamorphosis of the sometimes ugly and often bizarre caterpillar into an elegant butterfly also includes an ecological subtlety as the larva and adult are able to lead totally different life styles and thus avoid competing with each other for the same food.

The birdwing butterflies of southeast Asia are large and magnificently coloured. Of these the Queen Alexandra's birdwing butterfly (Ornithoptera alexandrae) is the largest with a wingspan of 10in (25cm). Its habitat is threatened by forest clearance.

which, in the case of the larger butterflies, may take several hours. The butterflies then mate, lay eggs and after perhaps only 6–8 weeks, finally die.

The largest butterfly in the world is the Queen Alexandra's birdwing, with a wingspan of perhaps 10in (25cm) or more.

The male butterflies have strangely shaped wings, rather like lobes and coloured with an exciting combination of shot green mingled with blue. The females, which are larger than the males, tend to be a duller brown colour with yellow gold flashes. They can be seen at various levels from the ground right up to the tree tops in the

Female butterflies usually lay their eggs on or near to the food plant on which the larva feeds. As the larva grows, it eats the yolk inside the egg and once hatched starts to consume the food plant on which it was laid. The larva or caterpillar grows quickly and has to shed its skin four or five times before it is fully grown. The larva is the main feeding stage in the life cycle and, when present in sufficient numbers, caterpillars can defoliate large areas of vegetation which can make them a serious pest if agricultural food is their main diet.

The end of the life of the caterpillar is marked by a final shedding of skin. During this period much of the larval tissue is remoulded to produce the adult body, particularly the wings, mouth parts and reproductive organs. The pupa or chysalis is immobile and, therefore, is particularly vulnerable to attack from predators. To prevent this the pupa may be covered by a silken cocoon (which is more common among moths) or protectively coloured to merge amongst certain plants.

When the adult is ready to emerge, the skin of the pupa splits behind its head, releasing the legs and antennae, followed by the rest of its body. The wings are soft and crumpled which is soon rectified by hanging them downwards, forcing blood into them. The wings then expand and are held apart allowing them to dry and harden

tropical rainforests of Papua, New Guinea. The butterflies will usually be found in the vicinity of flowers and certainly around rivers, streams, waterfalls and lakes. They prefer to fly at the edges of the forest and along paths or roads rather than through the dense undergrowth. Birdwings also fly high in the tree canopy, coming down only to feed.

The survival of butterflies worldwide depends on the protection of their natural habitat. Even though the Queen Alexandra's birdwing is protected in Papua, New Guinea, its fragile habitat is now seriously threatened by forest clearance for the development of the palm oil industry and other agriculture. WWF is mapping the exact distribution of this species and replanting the vines on which the butterfly feeds within designated reserve areas.

In some parts of the world successful butterfly ranching projects have been established whereby food plants are grown to lure wild butterflies into protected areas to lay their eggs. The pupae are collected and raised in cages, then some are sold to collectors and others released to boost wild populations. Usually, collecting butterflies in the wild does not endanger the insects unless the population of the butterfly is very small but it is still an unnecessary 'sport'.

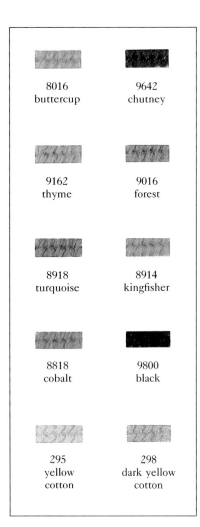

8016
buttercup

9642
chutney

9162
thyme

9016
forest

8918
turquoise

8914
kingfisher

8818
cobalt

9800
black

295
yellow
cotton

298
dark yellow
cotton

The Queen Alexandra's birdwing butterfly is the largest butterfly in the world but it is not the most colourful. The female is mainly brown and yellowy gold and I have tried to bring an iridescent effect to the wings by overstitching them with gold embroidery cottons. Other embroidery stitches could also be incorporated here and experimenting by using one stitch for the butterfly, another stitch for one coloured leaf and another stitch for other leaves would be fun.

The butterfly is a perfect shape for a round stool and to make the butterfly prominent I have designed a very soft background of yellowy green and blue vine leaves and grapes to represent the food of the larvae.

MATERIALS
Finished size: 11in (28cm) in diameter
Piece of 10-hole double thread canvas, 15 × 15in (38 × 38cm)
Anchor Tapisserie wools:
One skein each of 9800 black, 8016 buttercup
Two skeins each of 9642 chutney, 9162 thyme, 9016 forest
Five skeins of 8914 kingfisher
Short lengths of 8918 turquoise, 8818 cobalt
One skein each of Anchor stranded cottons, 298 dark yellow, 295 yellow

PREPARATION
1 Mark the middle of the canvas with horizontal and vertical lines of basting stitches.

WORKING THE EMBROIDERY
2 Follow the key and colour photograph to create this needlepoint design using half cross stitch throughout, except on the butterfly's feelers which are done in cross stitch, with the top stitch lying in the opposite direction to the rest of the embroidery. Over-stitch the wings with the yellow embroidery cottons. This provides the embroidery with additional texture and shine.

FINISHING
3 Press the design on the back with a steam iron gently pulling it back into shape (see page 105).
4 Attach the design to the footstool, ensuring the butterfly is centred correctly on the top. A staple-gun can be used to secure the edges or the edges can be laced together using a strong thread. Fold the corners neatly (see page 106). Cover the underside of the stool with a piece of fabric neatly slipstitched to the edges of the canvas.

TROPICAL RAINFORESTS

One of the most complex, beautiful and important ecosystems on this planet, the rainforests cover only 14 per cent of the land surface, yet hold at least half the world's species, most of them neither named nor studied.

There are many different kinds of rainforest. On high mountains areas cloud forests occur where mists envelop the shorter trees and their moss-covered branches. Further down the mountain, the trees become taller and various species grow, depending on the type of soil – either limestone or volcanic – or if they are near swampy ground such as the mangrove forests. The tropical lowland forests grow on comparatively dry ground and are the richest of all rainforests. Sadly they are also the most accessible and are therefore disappearing from all around the world.

There are many layers of life in a rainforest, although they are rarely apparent from the ground. Shrubs and creepers fill the floor of the forest, with small saplings growing through them on their way to the forest roof. Their leafy tops are dwarfed by the trunks of greater trees which hold their branches in the sun. Beneath this summit lies a network of stout branches creating a thick layer of limbs and leaves.

Light on the forest floor is at a premium, filtering through the canopy in tiny shafts. Small insects and butterflies follow the light which is soon relected or absorbed before reaching the leaves of the plants that live below. The growth of a new seedling can be interminably slow because of this, perhaps producing one or two leaves per year which are soon eaten by caterpillars. For the first 10 years of its life a hardwood seedling may not grow more than 3ft (approximately 1m) in height. The only opportunity for growth occurs when an old tree falls, leaving a huge hole in the canopy which floods the floor with hot, bright sunlight. Then there is instant

*The morning glory (*Ipomea*) climbing flower is one of 2 000 species found in rainforests. Many species have not yet been named.*

competition between all plants to reach the canopy level and survive. Within this canopy garden lives one of the richest animal kingdoms in the world with many insects living on just one tree, including such diverse creatures as a preying mantis disguised as an attractive pink bloom. In Panama, one tree was host to more than 1 200 species of beetles, 163 of which are found on no other kind of trees.

Many mammals and birds also live high up in the canopy. Pools provide nurseries for coloured frogs; hummingbirds maintain territories among gardens of hanging orchids and monkeys follow ancient routes through the branches in search of mates.

Hunter-gatherers and the tribes that practise a slash-and-burn agricultural system are the only humans who seem able to exploit the forest without destroying it. Over-hunting is rare where traditional methods are used and felling a few trees in order to create land for growing rice or maize does not cause long term damage as it provides time for the forest to regenerate. Damage only occurs when the forest has been burnt and destroyed over a large area and the land then used to grow crops such as coffee, which soon depletes the land of all nutrients. Ironically the rain forests occur in poor countries and there are good profits to be made in the short term. In Central America cheap beef reared on deforested lands is exported to the USA to be used as hamburgers in the fast food industry. Although this represents less than two per cent of American beef consumption, it has resulted in a quarter of the tropical forest in Central America disappearing forever.

The rainforests are millions of years old and should be protected, not only to save the countless plant and animal life living there but also to save the human race. Without the forests who knows what could happen to the world's climate in future generations?

8006 pearl	9522 cream
9552 wood	9562 marmalade
9640 nutmeg	9646 chocolate
8112 jasmine	9162 thyme
9100 spring	8992 grass

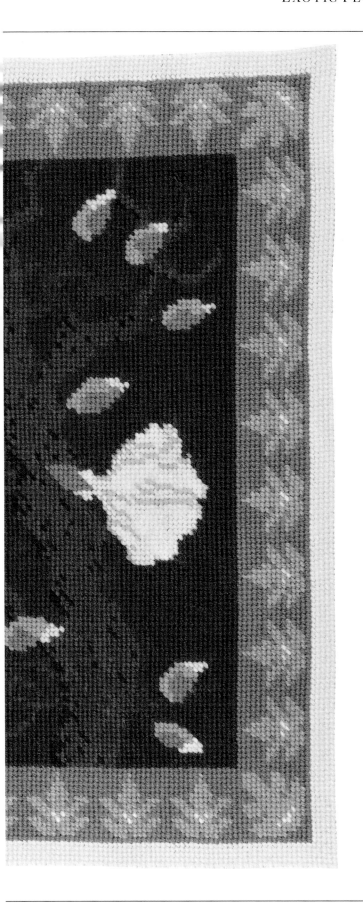

This design shows the *merremia vitifolia* which is only one of thousands of plants found in the tropical rainforests. Because the variety is to vast, I found it difficult to decide which plants to use. After sketching several designs, I decided upon this one, which is simple and uncomplicated.

Although the design has been made up into a cushion it can be easily adapted to a chair seat either by increasing the width of the yellow border or by extending the green background. Similarly, if the design is too large you could omit the leaf motifs in the border and reduce the width. The border could be abstracted and used to surround other designs, such as wallhangings, or it could make a bell pull just as it is.

MATERIALS
Finished size: 15¾in (40cm) square
Piece of 10-hole interlock canvas 20in (50cm) square
Anchor Tapisserie wools:
One skein each of 9522 cream, 9552 wood,
*   9562 marmalade*
Two skeins of 9646 chocolate
Three skeins each of 9640 nutmeg, 8112 jasmine,
*   8006 pearl*
Four skeins of 9162 thyme
Five skeins of 9100 spring
Six skeins of 8992 grass
Piece of backing fabric 19in (48cm) square
Cushion pad 16in (40cm) square

PREPARATION
1 Mark the centre of the canvas with horizontal and vertical lines of basting stitches.

WORKING THE EMBROIDERY
2 Following the key and the photograph, stitch the design, starting in the centre and working in half cross stitch throughout.

FINISHING
3 Press the embroidery on the back with a steam iron, easing the canvas back into shape if necessary. Leave to dry naturally.
4 With right sides together, sew the backing fabric to the embroidery on three sides.
5 Trim the excess canvas back to within ½in (12mm) of the embroidery.
6 Turn right sides out and insert the cushion pad. Close the open seam with slipstitch.

EXOTIC PARROTS

The parrot species covers a wide variety of birds including macaws, parakeets, lovebirds and parrotlets. There are great differences in shape and size, from the pygmy parrots of New Guinea which are less than 3½in (9cm) in length to the giant hyacincth macaws of South America which have a total length of approximately 40in (100cm) and are the largest of all parrots. Parrots also vary in plumage colouration. The majority are brilliantly coloured with shades of green, red and yellow predominating but there are dull coloured species like the Vasa Parrot from Madagascar. All parrots tend to live in the southern hemisphere, with Australia and tropical America being very rich in these birds while in Africa and tropical Asia they are quite scarce.

The majority of parrots are found in lowland tropical rainforest living in the forest canopy with their bright colours acting as a perfect camouflage while they feed. Some species, however, have adapted to higher altitudes with one bird, the kea, being found in the Southern Alps of New Zealand, where it can sometimes be seen rolling around in the snow.

Over the centuries the pet trade has brought many species of birds to near extinction and, today, as many as 8 million birds are being taken from the wild each year to supply the pet trade. Thirty parrot species are threatened with extinction, with western countries providing the main market for pet birds. The worst aspect of the trade is that the numbers brought into a country hide an enormous mortality rate. The birds that leave an exporting country alive represent only a fraction of those that were caught. Unknown numbers are killed or maimed during capture, or die before they can be shipped, and many more die in transit.

The Spix's macaw is the most endangered of all the parrots, its numbers being reduced to just one

*The brightly coloured scarlet macaw (*Ara nacao) *is found throughout Central America while the red-fronted macaw (*Ara rubrogenys) *is only found in a small area in Bolivia. They are both endangered.*

bird in 1990 by excessive trapping and habitat destruction. However, the high prices commanded by these birds will ensure that wild birds remain targets for trappers and dealers. There's a simple solution, however, as most birds caught in the wild can be bred in captivity and those that can't are probably not suitable as pets anyway.

However alarming the statistics seem, trapping is not the main cause for the decline in the parrot population. Habitat destruction has had a far more serious effect, especially with the widespread destruction of the tropical rainforests. Most parrots nest in holes in trees which are being felled by the logging companies resulting not only in the loss of their nesting sites but also their source of fruits and seeds.

The scarlet macaw is probably one of the best-known of all South American parrots and can be found in the Amazon basin and throughout central America. It is frequently depicted in travel brochures because of its attractive scarlet plumage and blue, yellow and green wings. However, because of the destruction of its forest habitat together with hunting, trapping and collecting of nestlings for the pet trade, an alarming decline in numbers has occured.

The red-fronted macaw is a little-known bird, though in the past few years it has entered the live-bird trade. It can be recognised by its olive plumage, blue wings and orange crown. Although not in immediate danger as a few thousand still live in Bolivia, it is disconcerting to find it being trapped at a time when international efforts are being directed towards limiting trade.

WWF is running parrot projects in South America where efforts are being made to stem the clearance of tropical forests and set up reserves. In Peru's Manu National Park, which WWF has been supporting for many years, seven different macaw species have their home.

8006 pearl	9800 black	8016 buttercup
9536 cinnamon	8218 cherry	8220 crimson
8594 violet	8612 indigo	8690 sapphire
8904 ultramarine	8990 emerald	8992 grass
9100 spring	9006 green	9154 peapod
9024 malachite	9196 lime	9168 olive
9216 khaki	9206 verdure	9640 nutmeg
	9646 chocolate	

I love the wonderful colours found in all tropical birds and I think these parrots make a striking firescreen design. The bright reds, oranges and blues look stunning against the deeper green of the foliage and the creamy white background makes the whole design very fresh.

Although the design looks complicated it is, in fact, quite simple to stitch. The birds' feathers look effective but are just outlines coloured in with a few stitches of extra colours to add depth. This technique avoids the involved task of mixing colours together to get a subtle shading, and because it is simple, it probably works better.

The leaves were fun to draw especially the large cheeseplant leaves at the bottom of the picture and also the vines curling down away from the branches. Of course, this design need not be used as a firescreen but could also make a wall-hanging. Or part of it could be stitched to make a cushion, perhaps the two parrots together on a branch with some foliage surrounding them.

MATERIALS
Finished size: 18 × 24in (46 × 61cm)
Piece of 12-hole interlock canvas, size 20 × 28in (50 × 71cm)
Anchor Tapisserie wools:
One skein each of 9154 peapod, 8016 buttercup, 9536 cinnamon, 8220 crimson, 8904 ultramarine, 8990 emerald, 9800 black, 9206 verdure, 8612 indigo, 9216 khaki, 9168 olive, 8594 violet, 9646 chocolate, 8690 sapphire
Two skeins each of 8218 cherry, 9640 nutmeg, 9196 lime, 9100 spring
Three skeins each of 9006 green, 9024 malachite
Four skeins of 8992 grass
Ten skeins of 8006 pearl
Firescreen to fit the finished work

PREPARATION
1 Mark the middle of the canvas with vertical and horizontal lines of basting stitches.

WORKING THE EMBROIDERY
2 Follow the key and photograph to work the design using half cross stitch throughout.

FINISHING
3 After completing the stitching, dampen the embroidery and pin it to a covered board, allowing it to dry naturally. Trim the unworked canvas to about 2in (5cm) from the edges then tack to the mounting board of the firescreen.

HEALING PLANTS

For many thousands of years plants have been the principal source of drugs used to cure all manner of illness. People all around the world, from very advanced civilizations to the most simple of cultures, have relied on plants to keep them healthy, and it is only recently, with advances in synthetic chemistry, that developed countries have broken their dependence on cures that came almost entirely from plants.

Despite the learning of such classical authorities as Dioscorides, whose *De Materia Medica* which was written in the first century AD and became the basis of European medicine for the next 1 400 years, expounding the virtues of some 600 different plants, the Dark Ages produced a long period of ignorance in Europe from which modern medicine only slowly emerged. People had no idea how plant cures worked and believed in ancient theories such as a heart-shaped plant leaf curing a heart affliction.

All plants produce chemicals for a range of different purposes but the plants of the rainforest are often the richest in defence chemicals for protection against predators and these chemicals are the raw materials for some of our most useful and potent drugs.

The bark of trees or vines often contains the highest concentrations of these defence chemicals. One example of this is quinine, the potent antimalarial drug found in the root and trunk bark of cinchona trees native to the humid forests of the South American Andes. It was first isolated in 1820 and was so successful in the treatment of malaria that demand for the drug almost wiped out the producer trees until mass production was made possible through a high-yielding strain which lent itself to cultivation.

Some other plant compounds have served as natural chemistry lessons, the essential items ultimately being manufactured synthetically. The aspirin story is a classic example. Dioscorides, again in his *De Materia Medica*, described the

The rosy periwinkle (Catharanthus roseus) *has certain compounds which are known to help cure childhood leukemia. It is one of at least 2 000 known species found in rainforests worldwide that have potential as curing cancer.*

white willow as a painkiller with the active ingredient being identified in the nineteenth century and named salicin. A similar compound was also isolated from meadowsweet and named salicyclic acid. In 1899, it was found that a mixture of this with acetic acid was more effective as a painkiller and the compound was named aspirin. It is now manufactured synthetically and is the most widely-taken medicine in the world.

The pretty rosy periwinkle is found in the tropical rainforests of Madagascar and is one of at least 2 000 flower species found in rainforests worldwide that have potential for curing cancer. At present, only one in ten of all tropical forest plants have so far been screened. The rosy periwinkle yields vincristine and vinblastine which, when used with other treatments, increases the success rate to 4 in 5 for the treatment of childhood leukemia.

If plants such as the rosy periwinkle, the two types of foxgloves, the cinchona tree and the white willow had become extinct before their chemical powers had been discovered, think how much extra human suffering would have endured. The 119 plant-derived modern drugs currently in use throughout the world are obtained from less than 90 species of plants. In contrast, in south east Asia, approximately 6 500, and in India 2 500, plant species are used by traditional healers. In China, 5 000 medicinal plants have been catalogued, of which some 1 700 are in common use. The plants in the rainforests are virtually untapped and are becoming extinct at a terrifying rate, resulting in a loss of biological diversity that will affect everyone on earth.

WWF is working to preserve this biological diversity through international laws and agreements, education and training, as well as the protection of habitats and species. The millions of plants, animals and micro-organisms are the result of 4 billion years of evolution and are vital for man's well-being.

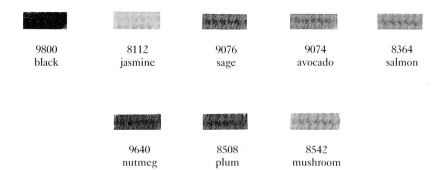

9800	8112	9076	9074	8364
black	jasmine	sage	avocado	salmon

9640	8508	8542
nutmeg	plum	mushroom

The rosy periwinkle is a familiar flower and may be grown by many people as a small pot-plant with either pink or white flowers. It is a member of the poisonous dogbane family and a relative of the hardy, evergreen creeping periwinkles which decorate many British gardens. Even though it does have anti-tumour agents these are in minute quantities in each plant and many plants are needed to make up a substantial amount of compounds.

It is a very pretty plant and I have used three of the flowers in this design to make a small needlecase. The same pattern is repeated on the front and back. The needlecase covers are lined with an attractive fabric, with a piece of folded felt sewn inside the covers to hold the needles.

The design could be used for a matching pincushion with perhaps only one of the flowerheads centred on the reverse side, or the motif could be repeated all over a larger piece of canvas to make a cushion. The two border rows of pink could be incorporated, or not, as you prefer. The colours could also be changed to white periwinkle flowers on a pink background. It is an adaptable design and it would be fun to experiment, making up several items all with a coordinating theme.

The pretty rosy periwinkle from the rainforests has the potential for successfully treating leukemia.

MATERIALS
Finished size $4\frac{1}{4} \times 4\frac{3}{4}in$ (11 × 12cm)
Two pieces of 12-hole interlock canvas, each 6 × 7in (15 × 18cm)
Anchor Tapisserie wools:
One skein each of 9076 sage, 9074 avocado
Two skeins each of 8364 salmon, 9800 black
Small lengths of 8112 jasmine, 8508 plum, 9640 nutmeg, 8542 mushroom
Two pieces of sprigged cotton fabric each $5 \times 5\frac{1}{2}in$ (13 × 14cm)
Piece of felt $4\frac{1}{2} \times 8in$ (12 × 20cm)

PREPARATION
1 Mark the middle of the two pieces of canvas with horizontal and vertical lines of basting stitches.

WORKING THE EMBROIDERY
2 Work two similar pieces following the key and the coloured photograph, using half cross stitch throughout and working outwards from the middle.

FINISHING
3 Press each piece of work on the back with a hot steam iron, gently pulling back into shape (see page 105).
4 Trim the unworked canvas to within $\frac{1}{2}$in (12mm) of the embroidery.
5 Fold the unworked canvas to the wrong side on both pieces.
6 With wrong sides facing join two long edges of the needlecase together using long armed cross stitch or over stitch.
7 Fold the edges of the cotton lining to the wrong side and slipstitch the lining to the wrong side of the needlecase.
8 Trim the felt edges with pinking shears, fold and sew inside the case, down the middle fold.

FORESTS
AND
PLAINS

The colours in temperate forests and plains are
very soft, consisting of shades of green,
brown and grey as opposed to the harsh, dry
colours of the safari landscape and the
strong, sharp colours of the tropical rainforests.
The animals, plants and butterflies I
have designed for this chapter all reflect the softer
tones. The wolves, bears and owl all
have warm colourings and have been designed to be
as realistic as possible with
the background detail more stylised.

THE NIGHT HUNTERS

Birds made their first appearance at the height of the dinosaur era. Today there are over 8 600 species of birds, divided into about 170 families with owls being classed as birds of prey.

Owls can be found all over the world, apart from some islands in the Pacific. Fluctuations in their numbers occur due to the availability of their food. However, their overall number is decreasing due to the disappearance of their natural habitat and contamination from the toxic chemicals in their food chain. Owls tend to be active at dusk and dawn, only a few hunt during the day. They are quiet and stealthy in their habits with specially adapted fluffy feathers for whisper-soft flight. Generally owls are distinguished by a large head (sometimes adorned with ear-tufts), a short neck, and strong and compact body with a fairly short tail. The plumage is normally rather drab except in the case of the snowy owl whose feathers are mainly white with dusty brown markings.

Some species of owl have a pair of still, horn-like ear-tufts which help to disguise the bird by breaking up the shape and outline of the head which might otherwise be too conspicuous. These tufts are sometimes referred to as 'ears' but they have nothing to do with hearing.

The eyes of a typical owl are large and placed at the front of the face so that the bird possesses a fairly wide field of binocular vision in the direction it is facing but has a very limited range of lateral vision. This, however, is compensated by the fact that the owl's head is remarkably flexible and is able to revolve through 270 degrees. The retina in the eye has special cells that are sensitive to light intensity, allowing the bird to see perfectly in the half-light of dusk or dawn.

It was long believed that owls managed to find their way in the darkness by means of sight alone. Although the retina of an owl's eye is also sensi-

The Seychelles Bare-legged Scops Owl (Otis insularis) is found in the hills on the island of Mahe in the Indian Ocean, where it is threatened by the destruction of its natural rainforest habitat.

tive enough to spot a mouse on the forest floor some distance away, even on a fairly dark night, ornithologists have now come to the conclusion that the owl is not primarily guided by vision. Rather, in fact, the bird will already have familiarised itself with every last detail of its hunting terrain so that it knows precisely the position and shape of each branch, rock and tree trunk within the territory. As the owl grows older the field of action is gradually extended but having explored an area thoroughly, nothing will induce it to venture farther into unknown territory.

Depending on individual size and weight, owls hunt a varied range of prey from insects to hares and rabbits. The largest part of the diet, however, usually consists of rodents and this is important in rural areas as it has a controlling influence on the rodent numbers which ultimately helps the farmer. The abundance or scarcity of rats, mice and other rodents in a particular district has a bearing on the bird's reproductive behaviour. When these small mammals are plentiful, the female owls lay a greater number of eggs and a larger proportion of young birds manage to survive the winter, as there is a good supply of food.

Owls in temperate climates tend to breed in late winter when it is still cold and when spring arrives the birds are ready and able to begin to catch prey. In the tropics and hot arid areas the pattern is rather different, but the general principle of gearing the reproductive cycle to the availability of food is maintained.

When they first emerge from the eggshell the owlets are tiny, blind, naked and helpless and are fed with extreme care on minute strips of flesh by the female who dismembers prey brought to the nest by the male. Fledging times vary widely from 20 to 30 days depending on the availability of food. Once the young have fledged, they are taught the skills of hunting by their parents.

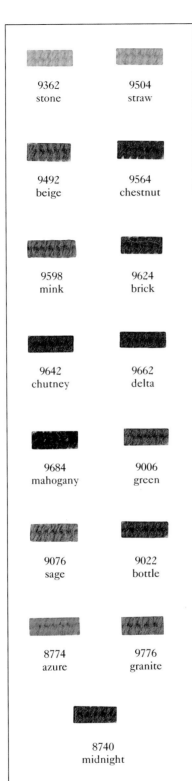

9362 stone	9504 straw
9492 beige	9564 chestnut
9598 mink	9624 brick
9642 chutney	9662 delta
9684 mahogany	9006 green
9076 sage	9022 bottle
8774 azure	9776 granite
	8740 midnight

This design shows the bare-legged scops owl which was thought to be extinct for many years. In 1959 a tiny population was rediscovered in the hills on the island of Mahe in Indian Ocean where its distinctive 'tock tock' call is often the only clue to its presence.

This design concentrates on the owl with the background a mass of leaves and beautiful blue flowers stitched on a deep midnight blue colour. The border is in the same colour tones but, if wished, a different blue border background could be used to make it more distinctive.

MATERIALS

Finished size 16 × 16in (41 × 41cm)
Piece of 12-hole interlock canvas 19 × 19in (48 × 48cm)
Anchor Tapisserie wools:
One skein each of 9662 delta, 9564 chestnut, 9076 sage, 9684 mahogany, 9624 brick, 9598 mink
Two skeins each of 9362 stone, 9504 straw, 9492 beige, 9776 granite, 9642 chutney
Four skeins each of 9022 bottle, 8774 azure
Five skeins of 9006 green
Ten skeins of 8740 midnight
Piece of backing velvet 18 × 18in (46 × 46cm)
Cushion pad 16 × 16in (40 × 40cm)
Thick upholstery cord 78in (2m) long

PREPARATION

1 Mark the middle of the canvas with horizontal and vertical lines of basting stitches.

WORKING THE EMBROIDERY

2 Stitch the design using half cross stitch throughout following the key colour and the photograph.

FINISHING

3 If the design has gone out of shape dampen it and pin it firmly onto a covered board, face downwards, allowing it to dry naturally back into a square (see page 105).
4 With right sides facing, sew the velvet backing to the embroidery along three sides.
5 Trim the excess material and canvas back to within ½in (12mm) of the embroidery. Trim the corners diagonally.
6 Turn right sides out and stuff with the cushion pad.
7 Close the fourth side with slipstitch.
8 Slipstitch the cord around the edges, making a loop at each corner if desired.

THE GREY WOLF

The largest members of the dog family, wolves have fascinated, terrified and commanded the respect of human beings for centuries. There are hundreds of stories of wolves in folk lore and mythology, from Aesop's Fables, the story of Romulus and Remus, the founders of Rome who were supposed to have been brought up by wolves, to werewolves who changed from men into wolves when a full moon shone at night.

The wolf was once the predominant predator of the northern hemisphere but the species is now rare, or extinct, in most places. Apart from Alaska and Canada, there are few wolves in the United States, and outside of Scandinavia and mountainous parts of eastern Europe they are rare. In Asia they can still be found in parts of China and Siberia. This decline in the wolf population is due to the destruction of forests to create farmland and man's indiscriminate hunting.

Wolves have been hunted for centuries. In the days when small villages were dependent on herds of sheep and cattle for food, a wolf taking a lamb or calf could mean starvation for the villagers. Traps, poison and guns were used to get rid the wolf and some dogs, such as the Irish wolfhound, were bred specially for this. Now, in countries where wolves still survive, wolf-hunting is carefully controlled or banned altogether.

Wolves are social animals living together in packs with a leader who sets the pace of the pack. When he moves the rest follow. He takes the initiative in pursuit and attack of prey and in the defence of the group. Fighting within the pack is rare although it can occur during the mating season.

Wolves rely on scent-making for communication but in the wilderness it is rare for wolf packs to meet each other. If another pack's scent is noticed it will be re-marked, assisted by howling to reinforce territorial rights. The pitches and

Now only to be found scarely scattered in the mountainous areas of eastern Europe, China, Siberia, Scandinavia and the USA, the European wolf (Canis lupus) is endangered due to man's hunting and the destruction of its natural habitat.

styles of calling differ among individuals and it is quite possible that members learn to identify each other by voice.

Coming from a long line of meat-eaters, the wolf is the descendent of a generalised carnivore, called the creodont, which lived in the northern hemisphere from 120–100 million years ago. Evolution has made the wolf a superb hunter and is probably the dog's closest ancestor, although the origins of domestic dogs are still unknown.

Wolves have a varied diet consisting of moose, deer and caribou (prey very much bigger than themselves) during the winter months with beavers, hares, mice, frogs and fish during the summer. When food is short they will eat snakes, worms, slugs and even grubs. When a wolf catches the scent of an animal, it trots upwind until it sees its quarry. Usually the scent of the prey will be followed from its tracks with the wolf stalking in a tense, alert manner. As with so many other land predators, they may be deterred by prey that approaches or stands its ground and it has been seen that adult moose and elk will usually bluff in this way. Normally the pursuit of prey will not exceed half a mile and they will not expend much energy in trying to catch very strong, swift prey, prefering to eat the old, young, sick or otherwise weakened member of a herd.

Wolves are not wasteful eaters. They feed first on the prime parts of their kill and then return later for the less desirable parts. What they do not eat immediately is buried. The entire digestive system of the wolf is geared to a feast and famine life – they eat every five or six hours when food is plentiful or can fast and live on scraps for two weeks.

Only the two strongest, dominant male and female wolves in the pack mate, and, after about nine weeks, as many as seven cubs are born. They are suckled until they are able to walk.

I found the wolves' faces very difficult to convert into needlepoint here, trying to make them 'wolf-like' and non-threatening at the same time. I originally saw the design in shades of grey but when looking at various photographs of wolves they all appeared much browner than expected. I did consider having shades of white representing a snowy scene for the background, but as the design is to be used as a footstool I thought this would be extremely impractical!

This design is very adaptable and can be used for a footstool, as shown here, a cushion, wall-hanging or a chair seat cover. The colours can be completely changed as well and, instead of the browny-greys, richer russets and chestnuts could be used on the animals turning them from a family of wolves into friendly dogs.

MATERIALS
Finished size 14½ × 14½ (37 × 37cm)
Piece of 10-hole double thread canvas 18 × 18in (46 × 46cm)
Anchor Tapisserie wools:
One skein each of 9442 magnolia, 9656 pepper, 9602 russet
Two skeins each of 9640 nutmeg, 9646 chocolate, 9014 spruce, 8712 blue-grey, 9776 granite
Three skeins each of 9638 dust, 9020 moss
Four skeins of 9016 forest
Short lengths of 9682 bonfire, 9372 putty
Footstool, 14in (35cm) square

PREPARATION
1 Mark the centre of the canvas with lines of horizontal and vertical basting stitches.

WORKING THE EMBROIDERY
2 Following the key and colour photograph and working from the middle, stitch the design using half cross stitch throughout.

FINISHING
3 Dampen the embroidery and pin it on to a board face downwards leaving it to dry naturally (see page 105).
4 Place over the footstool's cushion pad, making sure it is centred, and staple the unworked canvas to the board using a staple gun. Alternatively, lace the edges of the unworked canvas together firmly starting from the centre (see page 105).
5 Slipstitch a piece of material to the underside of the cushion pad to give a neat finish.

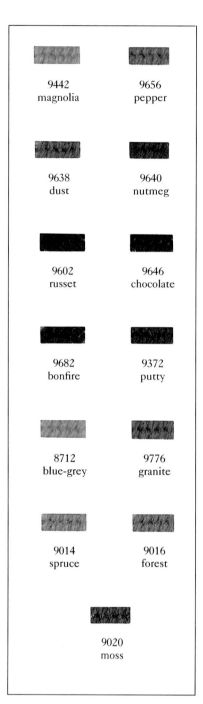

9442
magnolia

9656
pepper

9638
dust

9640
nutmeg

9602
russet

9646
chocolate

9682
bonfire

9372
putty

8712
blue-grey

9776
granite

9014
spruce

9016
forest

9020
moss

THE WILD ORCHIDS

The distribution of plants around the world can be traced back to the prehistoric age when the continents were joined as one land mass surrounded by sea. As the continents began to break and drift apart to become separated by ocean, plants began to evolve along individual lines. However, similarities can be seen between related species throughout the world.

Plants everywhere show an almost unbelievable diversity of shape, colour and form. A profusion of different patterns and colours with strong perfumes have all evolved and, in many cases, in association with insect pollinators particular to that part of the world. An example of this is the orchid with its curious flowers which mimic the insects in pattern and colour, and also in texture with the lip petal furry with soft hairs, like velvet. This attracts the pollinating insect to the flower.

Plants need to be pollinated to be able to produce seeds which will germinate, grow and ensure the survival of the species. The petals of the plants, which help attract insects, can open at any time of the year depending on factors such as the air temperature, the number of daylight hours and the enzyme reactions within the plant. As the days lengthen in spring, the bud-opening response in many plants is triggered and certain plants will flower.

Orchids are fascinating plants, having some of the most beautiful, colourful and incredibly bizarre flowers known to man. They grow all over the world with the majority of species occurring in the warm, humid tropics. However, some species can be seen in the Arctic circle in Alaska, Greenland and Siberia and others above the tree line on mountain ranges.

The flower is the most remarkable feature of an orchid. It may vary in size considerably from the

The development of land for farming has resulted in the declining numbers of the early spider orchid (Ophrys sphegodes).

tiny flowers of the *Pleurothallis* which are barely 2mm (0.08in) in diameter, to the flowers of the tropical American Brassia which may exceed 38cm (15in) in diameter.

The fantastic shapes, colours, textures and scents of orchid flowers are all designed with their respective pollinators in mind. Bees, wasps and humming birds are the most important pollinators of orchids. The colour and scent of each type of flower is cleverly designed to attract a certain type of creature to visit the flower. The flower structure guides and manipulates the pollinator so that the pollination mechanism may work with precision.

In general, orchids pollinated by bees have fragrant flowers with bright colours; those that attract moths are scented and light coloured with long tubular nectaries; butterfly-pollinated flowers are upright with fragrant colourful flowers, while bird-pollinated flowers are usually scentless. Orchids that attract flies often have dull brown or purple coloured flowers and produce odours that resemble decaying flesh!

The early spider orchid is pale green in colour with a brown and yellow lip. It may have up to six flowers blooming in spring. It is found in 17 locations on chalk down land in southern England, although it is declining due to arable cultivation and cattle grazing.

Wild orchids began to be collected extensively for cultivation during the nineteenth century when heated greenhouses became more efficient. This led to eventual over-collection, with some species of orchid endangered. However, they no longer have to be obtained in this way as orchids can be cultivated in greenhouses quite easily and many growers are constantly introducing new hybrids of species of very different origins which could not possibly occur in nature.

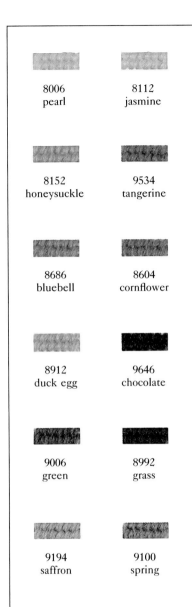

8006 pearl	8112 jasmine
8152 honeysuckle	9534 tangerine
8686 bluebell	8604 cornflower
8912 duck egg	9646 chocolate
9006 green	8992 grass
9194 saffron	9100 spring

This design is full of fresh flowers, reminiscent of long, hot summery days and would look perfect in a conservatory or a bright setting.

I have only used four different flowers but have designed them in such a way that they intermingle with each other. All the flowers are slightly stylised to give a strong shape.

This design easily be made larger by adding more background or even another row of border flowers or it could be made smaller by omitting the border. In this way the design could be used for a chair seat of any size. Details such as the orchid and its leaves, could make a spectacles case design or a strip consisting of the orchid plus the flowers above and below it could be repeated several times to make a bellpull. On finer mesh canvas the design could be used for a sachet.

MATERIALS
Finished size 14 × 14in (35 × 35cm)
Piece of 12-hole interlock canvas 18 × 18in
    (46 × 46cm)
Anchor Tapisserie wools:
One skein each of 8992 grass, 8152 honeysuckle,
    9534 tangerine, 9646 chocolate, 8112 jasmine,
    9194 saffron, 9100 spring
Two skeins each of 9006 green, 8604 cornflower,
    8686 bluebell, 8912 duck egg
13 skeins of 8006 pearl
Piece of backing velvet 17 × 17in (43 × 43cm)
Cushion pad 14 × 14in (35 × 35cm)
Upholstery cord 78in (2m)

PREPARATION
1 Mark the middle of the canvas with vertical and horizontal lines of basting stitches.

WORKING THE EMBROIDERY
2 Following the key and the colour photograph and working from the middle, stitch the design using half cross stitch throughout.

FINISHING
3 Dampen the embroidery and pin it face down on to a covered board, leaving it to dry naturally (see page 105).
4 With right sides facing, sew the backing velvet to the embroidery along three sides.
5 Trim the excess material to within ½in (12mm) of the embroidery cutting the corners diagonally.
6 Turn right sides out and stuff with a cushion pad.
7 Close the fourth side with slipstitch.

THE SPRING GENTIAN

During the last century, twenty species of wild flowers in Britain alone have become extinct and another 300 species are known to be endangered and under serious threat of extinction. This pattern is being repeated worldwide. In the last few decades increasing pressures threaten many wild plants, from changes in farming practices, land drainage, and hedge-clearance to the spread of towns and the building of new roads. The once common poppy, for example, which could always be seen during summer is now kept under control by pesticides and is, sadly, rarely seen.

Plants have taken millions of years to evolve and their development is closely linked to the great climatic changes of past eras. About 250 000 years ago a series of Ice Ages occurred, almost completely covering Britain with ice. At the edges of the ice sheet, plants colonised the land and as the ice advanced and then retreated, the vegetation varied from heathland to forest to arctic flora.

On mountain crags above the ice, plants which could tolerate sub-arctic conditions at high altitudes were able to survive. In Upper Teesdale in northern England, an arctic-alpine plant community can still be seen growing – an isolated pocket of vegetation which has survived from the Ice Ages until the present day. The spring gentian is one example of these 'relict' plants.

Following the Ice Ages Britain was covered by tundra, (a low arctic heath) with the ground frozen for much of the year but still able to support small plants and shrubs. These were mostly lichens and mosses, but small arctic flowering plants and berry-bearing shrubs, such as the bilberry, also managed to flourist. Tundra landscape still covers large areas of Scandinavia, Canada and arctic Russia today.

As the temperature gradually rose, the tundra was replaced by grassland and trees, juniper, birch

The blue-flowered spring gentian (Gentiana verna) is found in grassy places on limestone from April to June.

and pine with alder in wet places, and in time much of the land was covered by mixed oak forests. The land which was unsuitable for trees was covered by peat bogs. By around 5500 BC Britain had become a separate land mass surrounded by sea and the climate modified into the Atlantic climate with the vegetation evolving into the familiar plants which exist today.

Conservation of wild plants began at the turn of this century when the Society for the Promotion of Nature Reserves was set up in 1912 (now called the Royal Society for Nature Conservation).

By the middle of the twentieth century nature conservation began to strengthen worldwide and in Britain areas of particular scientific interest were given priority. These were primarily salt-marshes, shingle beaches and the marshlands in the Midlands as they were all recognised as characteristic types of wild country in Britain with no exact counterpart in continental Europe.

A national survey was published in 1962 by the Botanical Society of the British Isles. This listed all the wild plants in each area and showed those which were most threatened.

As a result of this research, it was agreed that legislation for the protection of plants was necessary and the Wildlife and Countryside Act 1981 became the law of the land protecting both habitats and individual plant species. It is now an offence in Britain to uproot any wild plant without the permission of the landowner, or to pick, uproot or destroy any protected plants.

Sir Maurice Abbot-Anderson, one of the first pioneers for plant protection, wrote in 1928, 'wild flowers, once picked, soon wither, and then give joy to no one, not even the picker; whereas if left to bloom, they are admired in their own surroundings by all who have eyes to see'. Sound advice indeed.

Spring Gentian Spectacles Case

8006 pearl	8296 shell pink	8672 china blue	8690 sapphire	9002 apple
9018 leaf	9074 avocado	9076 sage	8112 jasmine	

This flower is extremely striking with beautiful blue flowers among a mixture of green leaves and yellow and green stems. It is one plant species that has managed to survive since the Ice Age and, although very rare Britain, it is found on higher ground throughout Europe.

Because of its long and thin shape, I thought it would be ideal for a spectacles case. I used a soft peachy pink wool for the background to bring out the vivid blue of the flowers and highlight the subtle shades of green in the foliage. It is a quick project to complete, and even quicker if the back is lined with fabric rather than repeating the same needlepoint design.

MATERIALS
Finished size 4 × 6½in (10 × 17cm)
Two pieces of 12-hole interlock canvas 6 × 8in
  (15 × 20cm)
Anchor Tapisserie wools:
One skein each of 9002 apple, 9018 leaf
Two skeins of 8672 china blue
Three skeins of 8296 shell pink
Small lengths of 8112 jasmine, 8006 pearl,
  8690 sapphire, 9076 sage, 9074 avocado
Two pieces of pretty cotton lining fabric 5 × 7½in
  (12 × 19cm)

PREPARATION
1 Mark the middle of the two pieces of canvas with vertical and horizontal lines of basting stitches.

WORKING THE EMBROIDERY
2 Begin stitching in the middle of the canvas using half cross stitch following the key and the colours shown in the photograph. Make up two pieces of embroidery.

FINISHING
3 Press each piece on the back with a hot steam iron, gently pulling it back into shape (see page 105).
4 Trim the unworked canvas back to within ½in (12mm) of the embroidery, cutting the corners diagonally.
5 Put the two pieces of the spectacles case together, wrong sides facing and join on 2 long sides and the bottom edge using long armed cross stitch.
6 Stitch the lining pieces together, right sides facing, on the long sides and bottom edge. Trim the seam allowance. Slip the lining into the spectacles case. Turn in the lining and canvas on the open, top edge. Slipstitch together.

THE BROWN BEAR

At one time, the bear was a familiar inhabitant of the mountains and forests of Europe, Asia and North America, roaming regions where the summers were cool and there was a plentiful supply of water. Today, with the exception of the polar bear, the bear is restricted to a few remote hill and mountain districts and unfrequented forests. His decline has been due to the conversion of natural habitat to farmland and, more seriously, man's hunting of the bear.

Most of the 8 species of bear live in the northern hemisphere. The largest is the polar bear, followed in size by the brown bear, American black bear, Himalayan or Asian black bear, spectacled bear, sloth or honey bear, and the sun bear. The giant panda is now also classed as a bear.

Brown bears were once quite common in the northern countries of the world but are now scarce. In Scandinavia and eastern Europe a few thousand survive, while in North America the number has dropped to around 1 000 from a figure of well over 100 000 in 1800. Bears can still be found in the Arctic Circle, Alaska, Russia, Scandinavia and eastern Europe and wildlife experts have begun reintroducing the species into the Alps.

The brown bear varies tremendously in colour and size due to his ability to adapt to a wide range of surroundings, varying from sea level to altitudes of several thousand feet. He is an omnivore and can, therefore, take full advantage of all the food sources in a particular environment. A bear's diet consists of worms and larvae, bulbs, tubers and roots, currants, raspberries, bilberries and strawberries, pears, insects, small mammals, birds and fish. Honey and eggs are choice delicacies, if they are available. Water is important to the bear who drinks it in moderation but bathes in it frequently.

The brown bear goes into winter dormancy (as

Although hunted to near extinction and threatened by the destruction of its natural habitat, the brown bear (Ursus arctus) can still be found in arctic Canada and Alaska and some parts of Russia, eastern Europe, Scandinavia and USA.

opposed to true hibernation) by mid-winter. He finds a suitable cave and installs a litter made of grass and dead leaves which is so thick that when the animal is lying down his body is hard to detect. He covers the entrance with dry branches which can completely seal the cave after a heavy snowfall. During the ensuing winter months all the body functions are slowed down, especially the rate of heartbeat and breathing. The reserves of fat built up by feeding during the summer and autumn are now used as the bear will not feed again until spring.

At the end of the long winter sleep, the bear wakens and spends most of his time feeding, primarily on vegetation. By early summer the bear is strong enough to hunt and mate. Whereas the majority of male animals exhibit great boldness during the mating season, the bear seems to become more cautious and secretive than at any other time of the year. The male tends to mate with a previous partner and the gestation period of the female varies between 180–250 days. The birth takes place during the winter.

The newborn cub is a tiny, defenceless creature, weighing under 1lb (450g) and measuring only about 9in (22cm) long. Its diminutive size is probably due the mother's semi-lethargic condition, living off her reserves of fat. A larger cub would cause her to become exhausted, both in the process of giving birth and in suckling.

The number of cubs in a litter varies according to the age of the mother. Comparatively young females of 5 to 6 years will only have one cub, mature females two or three, and elderly females one or two. They are raised on an exclusive milk diet for about 3 to 4 months and then will venture out of the lair to experiment with other types of food. The cubs become adults at 3 or 4 years and it is only then that the mother is ready to mate again, usually with her previous partner.

This picture was great fun to design because the dark colours of the bears worked really well with the fruits around the border, giving the whole design an autumnal feel. The bears' fur is so thick and appears to be made up of hundreds of shades of colours all catching the light at different moments.

The border shows some of the fruits the bears would eat in their natural habitat – strawberries, raspberries, blackberries and blackcurrants – but almost anything could have been chosen as bears are not fussy about their food. This border design could be used time and time again around other needleworks or adapted for other designs such as a bellpull or spectacles case.

MATERIALS
Finished size: 11½ × 11½in (29 × 29cm)
Piece of 12-hole interlock canvas, size 15 × 15in
   (38 × 38cm)
Anchor Tapisserie wools:
One skein each of 9684 mahogany, 9490 walnut,
   8006 pearl, 8218 cherry, 8526 purple,
   8612 indigo
Two skeins each of 9646 chocolate, 9564 chestnut,
   9100 spring, 9490 walnut
Three skeins each of 9006 green, 8992 grass
Six skeins of 9450 spice
Short lengths of 8016 buttercup, 8392 pale pink,
   8548 lilac, 8420 raspberry
Mounting board and picture frame

PREPARATION
1 Mark the middle of the canvas with horizontal and vertical lines of basting stitches.

WORKING THE EMBROIDERY
2 Following the key and photograph, stitch the embroidery using half cross stitch throughout.

FINISHING
3 Press the embroidery on the back with a hot steam iron gently pulling back into shape. If it is has distorted dampen it and pin it into shape on a covered board leaving it to dry naturally (see page 105).
4 Place the embroidery over a mounting board and fold the canvas edges to the wrong side. Secure by lacing threads. Work first crossways and then lengthways starting at the centre and working to the corners (see page 105).
5 Place in a frame, with or without non-reflective glass, as required.

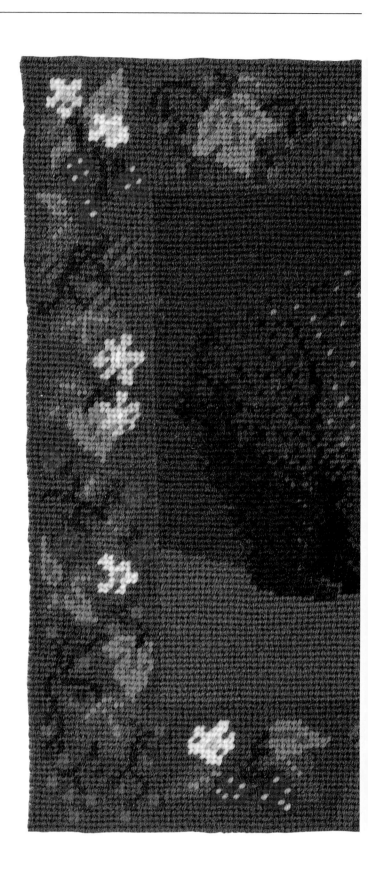

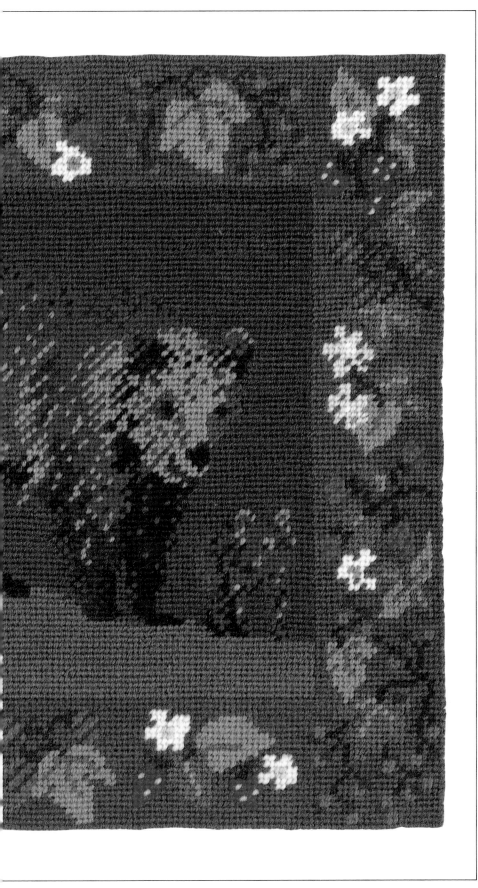

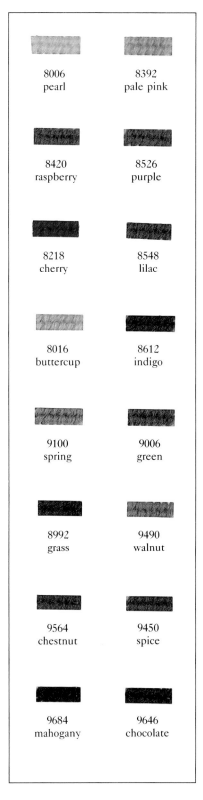

8006
pearl

8392
pale pink

8420
raspberry

8526
purple

8218
cherry

8548
lilac

8016
buttercup

8612
indigo

9100
spring

9006
green

8992
grass

9490
walnut

9564
chestnut

9450
spice

9684
mahogany

9646
chocolate

BEAUTIFUL BUTTERFLIES

Butterflies are among the most easily recognisable of all creatures. They are universally popular as they do not bite, sting or carry disease like other insects.

In Britain there are currently 57 resident native butterflies with several others that visit regularly and will breed if the conditions are right. This number is only a tiny fraction of what it was a century ago, and even 20 years ago butterflies were still a common sight in summer gardens and countryside.

Butterflies can be broadly split in two groups; those that prefer grassy downland areas and those that prefer leafy woodlands. The Adonis blue can be found on chalk downlands in isolated scattered colonies from the Chilterns southwards. Essentially a warmth-loving species, it is restricted to south-facing sun-traps where its larval food plant, the horseshoe vetch, grows in close-cropped grass together with an abundancy of ants, which are essential to the creature's survival.

Ants are particularly attracted to the Adonis blue. From caterpillar stage through chrysalis to the emergence of the butterfly, ants offer protection from other carnivorous ants and parasitic wasps. The attraction comes from nutritious droplets exuded from the caterpillar's honey-gland and skin, plus a strange rasping, barking noise which is especially apparent when the caterpillar crawls. The sound can arouse or pacify the ants depending on pitch.

The first brood of adults are on the wing from late spring to early summer, while the second brood is a late summer insect. The males are a brilliant metallic blue and are especially noticeable in bright sunshine. The females tend to be chocolate brown in colour with orange crescents.

The purple emperor, in contrast, prefers oak woodland areas and was once widely distributed throughout the midlands and the eastern and southern counties of England, with a few recorded sightings in Wales.

*There are currently only 57 resident native butterflies in Britain including the Adonis blue (*Lysandra bellargus*) and purple emperor (*Apatura iris*).*

Purple emperors rarely visit flowers, except the buddleia and the sweet chestnut blossoms, preferring to feed on a substance known as honeydew – the partly digested sap that has been secreted onto leaves by aphids. Sap is rich in sugars and is an important, high energy food for a range of insects. In addition to honeydew, the butterfly will also visit trees where sap may be oozing from a small wound. Salt is another important food for the male butterfly only and this can be found in moist ground or in animal droppings.

The adult purple emperor is on the wing from mid-summer. A few females emerge in early summer, followed by a mass emergence later when a high percentage of the males have established territories. This acts as an insurance against poor weather and is a characteristic that has evolved in many butterfly species that have had to adapt to climatic change over the centuries.

The main threat to the future of the purple emperor and the Adonis blue is the loss and fragmentation of the natural habitat through intensive agriculture, development and neglect. The utilisation of land for agricultural purposes has often led to the destruction of the important woodland edge with smaller trees, shrubs and lower growing plants. This is a sheltered micro-climate that encourages a wide variety of plant and animal species. The drainage of fen and woodlands and the reclamation of heath and moorland, plus the destruction of hedgerows and the heavy use of fertilisers, herbicides and pesticides, all destroy both butterflies and their foodplants.

Neglecting traditional methods of woodland management, such as coppicing and grazing, has led to many woods and grassy areas becoming overgrown, crowding out the butterflies.

All these factors, plus the collecting of butterflies, have brought about the decline in the butterfly population. They are the first to disappear when the bulldozers and tractors, fertilisers and pesticides – and pollution arrive.

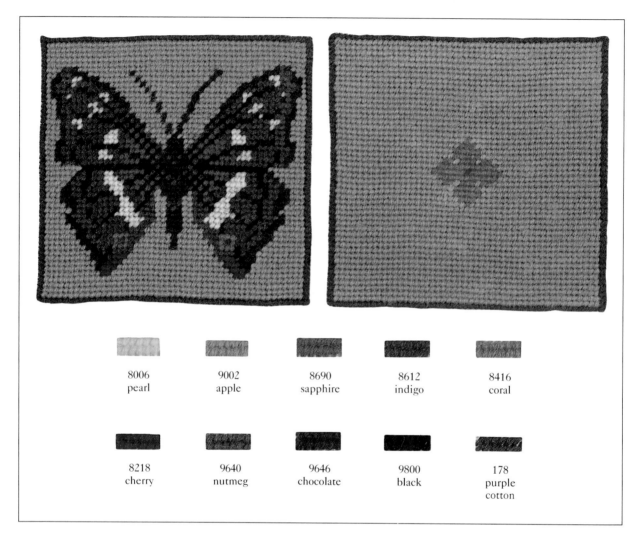

| 8006 pearl | 9002 apple | 8690 sapphire | 8612 indigo | 8416 coral |
| 8218 cherry | 9640 nutmeg | 9646 chocolate | 9800 black | 178 purple cotton |

These two little butterfly pin cushions are a delight to make. While stitching them I could remember the times spent picnicking in overgrown fields with many glorious butterflies dancing over the wild flowers, the air alive with movement.

I have tried to capture the brilliant colours of these particular butterflies by using stranded cotton on each. This, like the butterflies in the wild, is especially strong visually when it catches the sunlight.

On the pincushions' backs I have put a motif which is relevant to each butterfly. The reverse of the purple emperor butterfly pincushion has a pinky red buddlia flower which, in life, has many blossoms on a flower head and is much smaller than this. One the back of the Adonis blue pincushion I have stitched a sprig of horseshoe vetch which is the butterfly's larval plant. However, the backs need not be embroidered and a piece of pretty fabric could be used instead.

All four designs could be stitched on to one piece of canvas, adding a few rows for a border, to make a pretty picture. The designs are also ideal for a herb pillow if it were backed with a piece of wild silk and then stuffed with some lavender. Each of the designs could be miniaturized on 18-hole canvas to make a little picture or a box top.

MATERIALS FOR THE PURPLE EMPEROR
Finished size: 4 × 4in (10 × 10cm)
Two pieces of 12-hole interlock canvas 6 × 6in (15 × 15cm)
Anchor Tapisserie wools:
One skein each of 8612 indigo, 9800 black
Three skeins of 9002 apple
Short lengths of 8006 pearl, 9646 chocolate, 8690 sapphire, 9640 nutmeg, 8416 coral, 8218 cherry
Anchor stranded cotton:
One skein of 178 purple
Toy stuffing

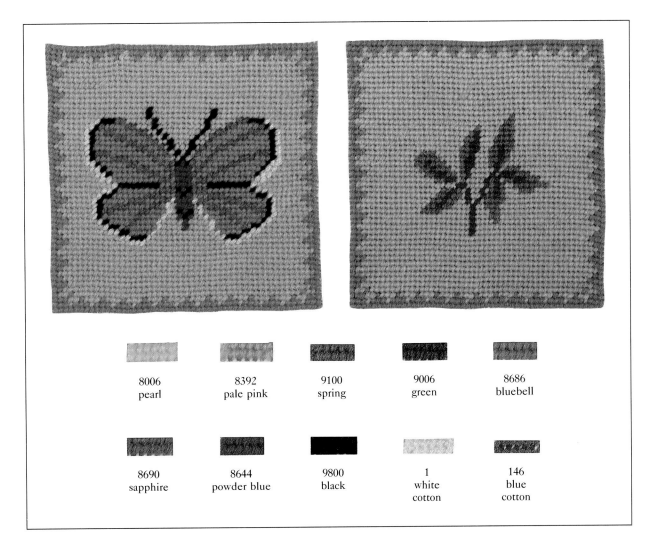

| 8006 pearl | 8392 pale pink | 9100 spring | 9006 green | 8686 bluebell |
| 8690 sapphire | 8644 powder blue | 9800 black | 1 white cotton | 146 blue cotton |

MATERIALS FOR THE ADONIS BLUE
Finished size: 4 × 4in (10 × 10cm)
Two pieces of 12-hole interlock canvas 6 × 6in (15 × 15cm)
Anchor Tapisserie wools:
One skein of 8686 bluebell
Three skeins of 8392 pale pink
Short lengths of 9800 black, 8644 powder blue, 8690 sapphire, 8006 pearl, 9006 green, 9100 spring
Anchor stranded cotton:
One skein of 1 white, 146 blue
Toy stuffing

PREPARATION
1 Mark the middle of each piece of canvas with vertical and horizontal lines of basting stitches.

WORKING THE EMBROIDERY
2 Follow the key and colour photographs to stitch the designs using half cross stitch throughout.

Begin in the middle working outwards, finishing by stitching the border. Stitch the design using the wool first and then over-stitch with the stranded cotton.

FINISHING
3 Press pieces gently using a hot steam iron to ease back into squares.
4 Trim the unworked edges of the canvas to within ½in (12mm) of the embroidery, cutting the corners diagonally.
5 With wrong sides together, sew the back and front of the pincushion together using long armed cross stitch or over-stitch to provide a neat finish. Start about one-third along one edge and then stitch around the four corners leaving a gap through which to stuff the pin cushion. Push the stuffing well down into the corners. You can use a knitting needle for this, or a blunt pencil tip. Stuff fairly firmly. After stuffing, the gap can be closed by continuing the long armed cross stitch.

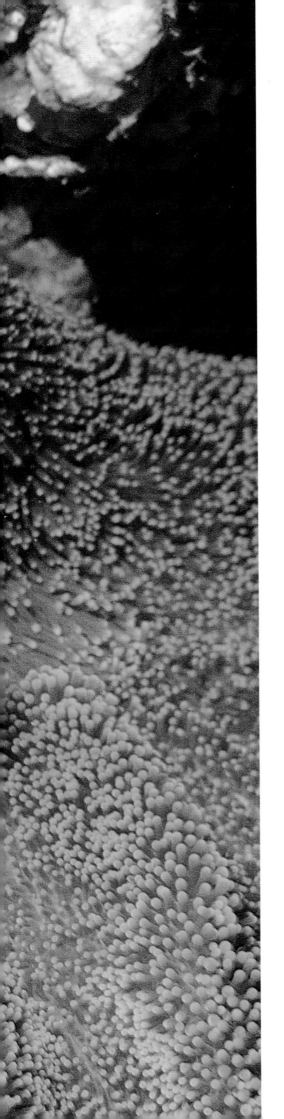

OCEANS
AND
WETLANDS

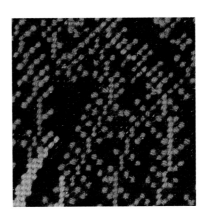

*The creatures that live in the seas and oceans and
the wetlands vary enormously. In the
warm, shallow seas, brilliantly coloured fish swim
among corals, ranging from bright pink
to dull brown in colour. In other parts of the
ocean, whales, dolphins and turtles live,
surviving by adapting to the changing environment
over thousands of years of
evolution. I hope the damage done to the seas and
wetlands by man will not cause these
beautiful and diverse creatures to become extinct.*

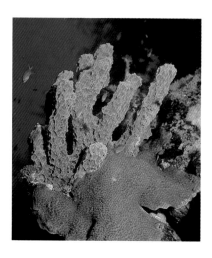
THE CORAL SEAS

The seas make up over 70 per cent of the Earth's surface with every stretch of water filled with life. Of all these different habitats the coral reef stands out because of the richness of species and the variety of shapes and colours it houses.

Stony corals are found in warm seas, and although solitary corals can be found in most oceans, it is only in warm waters that reefs will form. Coral reefs are composed of mainly 'dead' limestone with a thin surface covering of living coral made up of algae and polyps. The coral polyp has a simple structure of a soft cylinder of tissue, closed at the bottom with a mouth surrounded by tentacles at the top which, like its relation the jellyfish, contains tiny stinging cells. Inside is an open stomach cavity which is connected to other polyps in the colony so that if one catches food, they all benefit. It feeds by extending its tentacles and paralysing passing prey, such as a shrimp or an early larval stage of another reef animal, which it then passes down to its mouth. The prey is broken down in the polyp's stomach and the nutrients are passed to the whole colony.

Coral polyps create the living structures, known as coral colonies, by producing a skeleton of limestone and then dividing to form new polyps on top of this skeleton. Thus a continuous series of new levels is created and the stem of coral grows towards the light. The algae is important as it uses the sunlight to process carbon dioxide and the nitrogenous decomposition products of the polyps to produce oxygen. It also helps to cement together the skeletons of corals and other reef creatures to form a hard pavement of reef crests.

The warmer the water, the greater the variety of coral, and in turn, the more variety there is of other creatures that depend on the coral for food, a place of refuge, a hiding-place and a home. Fish, worms, starfish and molluscs all live there

Coral seas are to be found throughout the world in shallow waters with the largest variety of shapes and sizes occuring in warm seas. Many have already been damaged or destroyed and are all in danger from the threat of global warming.

in such close proximity that almost every tiny space is occupied. Many of the creatures have become specialized in eating the coral polyps. The brightly coloured parrot fish, for example, bites off the coral shoots and gnaws at the coral blocks with its specially developed hard mouth.

The corals in the Third worlds have declined for a number of reasons the main one being through natural causes such as hurricanes and disease. In Porto Rico, hurricanes in 1963, 1969, 1979 and 1980 caused great damage to the reefs and in 1984 a natural disease also destroyed parts of them. Unnatural causes, mainly brought about by man, have also damaged coral reefs. In Brazil, Columbia, Costa Rica, Venezuela, Indonesia and Malaysia, soil run-off due to logging and slash and burn agriculture clogs the coral polyps. In India, Sri Lanka and the Maldives coral is mined and used for the building of roads which is a serious threat to the coral.

Fortunately, several other reefs around the world survive, including the Great Barrier Reef of Australia. Here, during the late 1960s and early 1970s, public concern for the future of the reef became widespread resulting in the Great Barrier Reef Marine Park Act being passed in 1975, ensuring the future well-being of the Reef through the establishment of a marine park. This not only protects the reefs and their environments but also brings in revenue in tourism.

There is, however, recent evidence that global warming may pose a further threat to coral reefs. If sea temperatures rise too high, coral species cannot survive. If sea levels rise, some corals may 'drown' because they can only survive near the surface.

I have been lucky enough to swim in a coral sea and was fascinated by all the vividly coloured fish living in the coral. When they swim through the coral polyps with the sunlight filtering through the water the fish seem to disappear.

There are so many colours in coral seas it was difficult to choose the shades for this design, but I think the strong blues, pinks, yellows and apricots work very well together, especially against the black background. I have used a mixture of half cross stitch and cross stitch both in the border and in the main part of the design.

MATERIALS
Finished size: 15 × 15in (38 × 38cm)
Piece of 10-hole double thread canvas 19 × 19in (48 × 48cm)
Anchor Tapisserie wools:
One skein of 8690 sapphire
Two skeins each of 8114 daffodil, 8454 fuchsia, 8526 purple, 8234 rust, 8938 aqua, 8232 apricot, 8202 scarlet, 8808 peacock
Three skeins of 8644 powder blue
Five skeins of 9800 black
Piece of backing velvet 17 × 17in (43 × 43cm)
Cushion pad 15 × 15in (38 × 38cm)

PREPARATION
1 Mark the middle of the canvas with horizontal and vertical lines of basting stitches.

WORKING THE EMBROIDERY
2 Work the embroidery following the key and the colour photograph, making sure you note the differences between half cross stitches and cross stitches. On all the cross stitches, the top stitch runs in the opposite direction to the half cross stitch (this can be seen clearly on the fish's body). Cross stitch is also used on the coral's waving polyps and in the centre cross of each coloured square in the border.

FINISHING
3 Press the embroidery on the back with a hot steam iron allowing it to dry naturally (see page 105).
4 With right sides together, sew the velvet backing and the embroidery together on 3 sides.
5 Trim the seam allowances back to within ½in (12mm) of the embroidery.
6 Turn right sides out and stuff with the cushion pad.
7 Finish by closing the open seam with slipstitch.

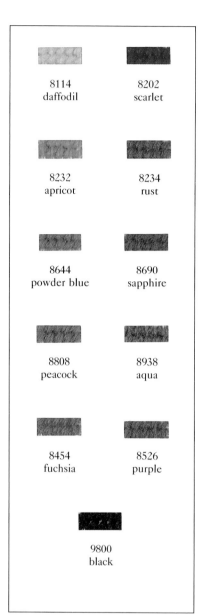

8114
daffodil

8202
scarlet

8232
apricot

8234
rust

8644
powder blue

8690
sapphire

8808
peacock

8938
aqua

8454
fuchsia

8526
purple

9800
black

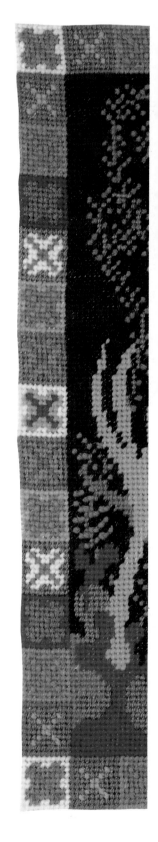

CORAL SEAS CUSHION

WETLANDS BIRDS

Birds are so diverse that they are able to live in all habitats – woodland areas, mountains, moorlands, lakes and rivers, wetlands, estuaries, coasts, islands, farmland, parks and towns. Each species of bird has evolved to make the best use of its environment.

The crane prefers the wetland areas ranging from upland peatlands to rivers, reed beds, wet grasslands and estuaries. These areas tend to be safe from predatory mammals as few land mammals swim and those that can, such as the otter and mink, commonly feed more on fish and other aquatic life than on birds.

Birds of the wetlands are often nomads, flying large distances in search of fresh water. Some, like the flamingos of East Africa, may patrol a string of lakes for years before they find one at the right stage for

The black crowned crane (Balearica pavonina) *lives in the open swamps, marshes and grasslands of Africa, from Senegal to Central Ethiopia, North Uganda and North-west Kenya.*

———————— • ————————

white-naped, hooded and Japanese cranes in Japan has dramatically increased the numbers of all three species in the last 25–30 years. Their feeding stations have become popular attractions for the public, whose knowledge and appreciation of the birds is increased by nearby visitors' centres. There are, however, risks in attracting a whole population of endangered birds to one place at one time as diseases can be transmitted.

Cranes have great cultural significance on all 5 continents where they occur. In the United States, the whooping crane is perhaps the symbol of all endangered species, while in Japan and China these graceful birds have long been a favourite subject for painters. There are 14 species of cranes but worldwide their populations have declined drastically

breeding. For others, migration between nesting grounds and wintering areas is predictable and for residents and visitors alike the wetlands are an essential part of life. A threat to one of their habitats translates immediately into a threat to many individual species.

Many endangered species of the wetland areas are large, long-lived birds with a low reproductive rate. They may not begin to breed until they are four or five years old, producing only one or two eggs a year. This rate can decrease even more if there is a shortage of food at the critical time of year. Both these causes can be helped by man's intervention by getting the birds to lay more eggs than usual.

The eggs are removed from wild pairs – either immediately after laying or when the clutch is complete – and are incubated artifically or under a broody hen. The original pair replaces its lost clutch, thus doubling its output of eggs. Extra supplies of food can be given to the birds during critical periods. Organised winter feeding of

in recent years. The primary cause has been the destruction of wetlands which are drained and used for agriculture, with hunting as a contributory factor.

China has 8 crane species, 5 of which are endangered. WWF is helping the Chinese government with wetlands conservation projects where black-necked, white-naped and Siberian cranes are found. The projects will not only benefit cranes but also a wide variety of other birds and wetlands animals.

Each year the Gallocanta lake in Spain is visited by 50 000 common cranes, three-quarters of the western European population of the species. Here WWF is involved in a campaign to prevent the growing conflict between cranes and local farmers angered by damage to crops. In Kenya, crowned cranes breed in marshes where their presence is a good indicator of water quality. WWF is focusing on these birds to develop a conservation strategy and management plan for threatened wetlands and bird species throughout East Africa.

Cranes and other marshland birds are exceptionally beautiful. I could watch them for hours, their long legs making them look so fragile and delicate and their heads continually bobbing up and down, picking up insects and grubs with their long beaks.

There are many crane species, with the whooping crane being the most endangered. However, I decided to design this spectacle case using the black crowned crane as I loved the delicate arrangment of spikes on their heads and the continuation of the same colour on their backs. I have used a fine 14-hole canvas to capture the detail on the birds, bringing in the vivid red and bright yellow colours but still making the birds look fragile.

The small black crowned crane in the design has the browny colour feathers of a young bird rather than the black and grey of the adult. He does, however, have the beginnings of a yellow crown and the red tail feathers and throat.

Because this design has been created on a fine canvas, it would be easy to enlarge by stitching it on a coarser 10-hole double thread canvas to get a design $5\frac{1}{2} \times 9$in (14×23cm). Two of these sewn together on three sides would make an evening pouch bag which could be closed by a zip-fastener on the top edge. Over-working some of the colours, such as the yellow and red, with stranded cotton adds an extra sheen and texture, ideal for an evening accessory.

MATERIALS
Finished size 4 × 6½in (10 × 17cm)
Two pieces of 14 hole interlock canvas, 6 × 9in (15 × 23cm)
Anchor Tapisserie wools:
One skein each of 9006 green, 9794 grey
Two skeins of 9002 apple
Three skeins of 8774 azure
Short lengths of 9658 smoke, 8114 daffodil, 8238 flame, 8006 pearl, 9800 black, 9768 charcoal, 9774 cloud
Two pieces of lining fabric 5 × 8in (13 × 20cm)

PREPARATION
1 Mark the middle of the two pieces of canvas with horizontal and vertical lines of basting stitches.

WORKING THE EMBROIDERY
2 Follow the key and the colour photograph, embroider the two sides of the spectacles case, using half cross stitch throughout.

FINISHING
3 Press the pieces on the back with a hot steam iron gently pulling them into shape (see page 105).
4 Trim the unworked canvas to within ½in (12mm) of the embroidery, cutting the corners diagonally.
5 With wrong sides together, join the two long sides and the bottom of the spectacles case with the 9006 green yarn using long armed cross stitch.
6 Stitch the lining pieces together on 3 sides, wrong sides facing. Trim the seam allowance and insert the lining into the spectacles case. Turn in the top edges of lining and canvas and slipstitch together.

8006 pearl	8114 daffodil	9774 cloud
9794 grey	9768 charcoal	9800 black
9002 apple	9006 green	8774 azure
9658 smoke	8238 flame	

WHALES AND DOLPHINS

Whales, dolphins and porpoises are known collectively as 'cetaceans', from the Latin *cetus* (a large sea animal) and the Greek *ketos* (a sea monster). Like man, they are warm blooded, air-breathing mammals that mate, give birth to live young and suckle their young on milk over a period of many months. Unlike man, they never venture on to land but live entirely in the water.

All cetaceans are streamlined with a perfect body shape for living in water. They are not dependent on their eyesight for survival, relying more on other senses, especially hearing as sound travels faster and further in water.

Other senses, such as touch and taste, are also important but the sense of smell, however, has been lost by the toothed whales, dolphins and porpoises.

The only significant predators of cetaceans, other than man, are sharks and the killer whale, false killer whale and pygmy killer whale. Generally these will attack the young rather than the larger adults. Man has hunted the whale for many years, mainly for its oil and meat and has contributed to a significant decline in all the different species bringing many to the brink of extinction.

The worst hit species were initially the slower, larger whales, such as the sperm whale and right whale, which had a high oil yield. The grey whale became a target in the early nineteenth century and the rorqual whales in the latter part of the century. Thereafter, blue, humpback, fin and sei whales were killed in their hundreds of thousands worldwide, especially in the Antarctic. The smaller minke whale only became a worthwhile quarry after these large species could no long support the industry.

The numbers of the endangered blue whale, the largest animal on earth, have now fallen below 10 000. In 1985 a moratorium on commercial whaling came into force but a few nations want to continue hunting whales, believing that stocks of

The humpbacked whale (Megaptera novaeangliae) *is found in temperate waters. It spends the summer feeding in cold-water areas, the winter in warm-water breeding grounds.*

some species are still numerous. However, WWF is strongly opposed to this as whale stocks have so far shown little sign of recovery from their depleted state and cetaceans are slow to reproduce, producing only one calf after a gestation period of 12–16 months.

Dolphins have been killed in vast numbers by being caught up in nets where man has been fishing for tuna. For some reason, which is not yet understood, yellowfin tuna swim directly underneath schools of dolphins. Fishermen have known this for years and have taken advantage of it to locate the fish. In 1959 the fishing industry went through a radical change, turning to synthetic nets and hydraulic machinery enabling whole schools of dolphins to be drawn into nets, catching and killing both tuna and dolphins. Despite the very high mortality over the last 30 years, none of the dolphin species involved is considered in immediate danger, although pollution and over-fishing are putting additional pressure on these marine mammals.

This is a different story to the river dolphins. Throughout the world industrial and agricultural development is degrading river systems. In India the Ganges river dolphin is under threat, and so is the boto or Amazon river dolphin which is a victim of the rapid loss of tropical rainforest.

The baiji river dolphin is the most endangered member of the cetaceans with only about 300 remaining in the Yangtse river in China which is constantly being polluted by industrial and agricultural effluent. Dams are being constructed which pose another threat and ships' traffic is doubling every ten years, resulting in the deaths of some dolphins due to vessels' propellors.

The baiji is protected from killing by law and WWF is helping the Chinese authorities to define the movements of the baiji along the river so that reserves can be set up. WWF is also helping the Chinese to conduct an awareness campaign among local fishermen.

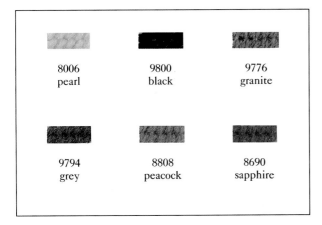

8006 pearl	9800 black	9776 granite
9794 grey	8808 peacock	8690 sapphire

This design took quite a long time to create as the whales and dolphins have very similar shapes and do not have particularly interesting colours. I originally wanted to create a general view of sea life as a cross-section with whales, dolphins and fish in the sea and seals and turtles on the land. However, because all the creatures are very streamlined in shape, and apart from the killer whale, have few exciting markings on them, it made them difficult to incorporate into a colourful needlepoint design.

I decided to keep to a very simple stylised design but create a mass of movement in the background which would bring attention to the mammals by their contrasting simplicity. The sea uses only two colours of blue and turquoise but mixing them in this way gives a wonderful swirling effect and helps to make the finished picture visually interesting.

This design could easily be adapted to make a rug for a child's room. A coarse canvas of 5-holes to 1in (2.5cm) would increase the size to 28 × 35in (71 × 89cm). Double the yarn in the needle otherwise the canvas will not be covered properly.

MATERIALS
Finished size 14 × 17½in (36 × 44cm)
Piece of 10-hole double canvas size 18 × 22in (46 × 56cm)
Anchor Tapisserie wools:
Two skeins of 9776 granite, 8006 pearl
Three skeins of 9800 black
Eight skeins of 8808 peacock
Ten skeins of 8690 sapphire
Short length of 9794 grey
Lining fabric 15 × 19in (38 × 48cm)
Two pieces of dowling, each 13½ × 1in (35 × 2.5cm)
20in (50cm) length of cord
Silky tassels (optional)

PREPARATION
1 Mark the middle of the canvas with horizontal and vertical lines of basting stitches.

WORKING THE EMBROIDERY
2 Following the key and the colour photograph and working from the middle, stitch the design using half cross stitch throughout.

FINISHING
3 Dampen the embroidery and pin it face downwards on to a covered board, leaving it to dry naturally (see page 105).
4 Place one piece of dowling along the top edge of the design and the other across the bottom.
5 Carefully attach the dowling to just inside the top and bottom edges of the embroidery by looping sewing thread around and catching the needlepoint. This will add weight to the wallhanging and make it hang properly.
6 With wrong sides together, sew the lining to the embroidery around all four sides using slip-stitch.
7 Attach the cord to the top corners of the wallhanging, adjusting the length to your own requirements. If the effect suits your furnishings, you might try adding silky tassels to the top corners of the wallhanging.

Up to 1973, the greatest number of Common Dolphins slaughtered were those killed for their oil and flesh off the Turkish coast.

THE WATER BIRDS

Birds have evolved over millions of years from scaly, flying reptiles into some of the most varied, beautiful and graceful creatures in the animal world. They have adapted into about 9 000 species which are able to survive in a wide variety of habitats, ranging from ice-cold seas to baking deserts.

The British Isles has a remarkably diverse variety of bird habitat for so small an area, due to the interaction between the climate, the geology and human management of the land – the factors deciding which plants can grow. These plants form the basis of the food chains on which birds and animals depend.

Britain's climate is well suited for long growing seasons due to the Atlantic weather system and the influence of the Gulf Stream, with mild, moist summers and protection from extreme, continental cold winters. Its varied geology influences the shape of the land and the fertility of the soil, affecting the growth and range of plants. The climate and geology have also produced a diversity of wetland habitats such as the tumbling upland streams which have few plants but many insects and are ideal homes for birds. The great fens of East Anglia are alive with wildfowl living off insects and plants in the vast reed beds and the estuaries hold flocks of waders probing for food in the mud. The coastal waters have many kinds of seafowl feeding off the teeming waters.

It is in the countryside that man has had the greatest influence on plant growth. About 6 000 years ago Neolithic man began to clear forests for grazing and crops which greatly increased the variety of habitats available to birds. Although this was good for some birds, the deforestation meant that some special habitats disappeared, leading to the extinction of the species that relied on them for food, for example the honey buzzard which fed on the grubs in wasps' and bees' nests only found in wild forest areas.

By Roman times over half of England's tree cover had been cleared and replaced by farmland.

The British red-throated diver (Gavia stellata) is now threatened with extinction due to its vulnerability to oil spills and lack of food caused by over-fishing for the commercial market.

Birds such as grey partridges, stone-curlews and great bustards began to settle and breed, finding plenty of food in the open coutryside. Where the forests were cleared but the soil was too infertile to farm, heathland grew creating the right environment for linnets, whinchats and pipits. Open land in high rainfall areas, as in Ireland and the British uplands, became moorland, clad in heathers, where red grouse, golden plovers and hen harriers spread and thrived.

The large-scale draining of wetlands and the new, huge conifer forests have altered the face of the uplands, and farming technology now makes much of the lowlands a difficult place for birds to live in. The variety of habitats and birds that remain are a testimony to the adaptability of so many species in the face of human pressure.

One of the British seabirds that is now in danger of extinction is the red-throated diver. It is the smallest diver to be found in the British Isles and is one of the rarer breeding birds. Its decline is attributable to lack of food due to overfishing for the commercial market and the bird's vulnerability to oil pollution – around 500 spills are reported off Britain's coasts each year.

The largest population of these birds is found in the Shetland Islands, nesting in small inland lochs or peat pools. Although the red-throated diver nests on these pools the adult birds have to fly many miles to find their food at sea or in lakes containing fish.

The clutch of one or two eggs is laid in a nest scrape close to the water's edge, or occasionally on a built-up platform in shallow water. Sometimes the nests are a mere cushion of aquatic vegetation often so close to water that, on large lochs, where strong winds can whip up large waves, eggs are often swamped. In late summer adults and young birds from the far north start moving a few hundred miles south where they stay until spring either in large, loose groups, singly or in pairs.

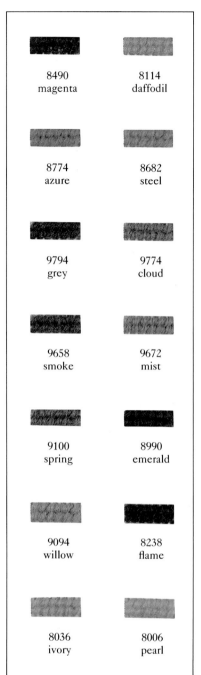

8490 magenta	8114 daffodil
8774 azure	8682 steel
9794 grey	9774 cloud
9658 smoke	9672 mist
9100 spring	8990 emerald
9094 willow	8238 flame
8036 ivory	8006 pearl

Birds of every species are interesting to draw as they have so many colours in their feathers and are a variety of different shapes and sizes. The shape of the red-throated diver is ideally suited to a tea-cosy and its warm grey-brown plumage and the flash of red on its throat contrast with the green foliage and the scattering of bright flowers on the blue water. I have purposely used quite a selection of colours to ensure the finished tea-cosy matches many tea services!

The quantities of wool given for this design are enough to stitch one side only. The reverse of the tea-cosy can be stitched with the same design or just in plain blue yarn. The needlework could also be backed with a piece of pretty cotton fabric. The cosy is lined inside with a piece of wadding covered in a washable fabric cut slightly smaller than the outer embroidery.

Egg-cosies can be made to coordinate with this design using yellow flowers on blue ground.

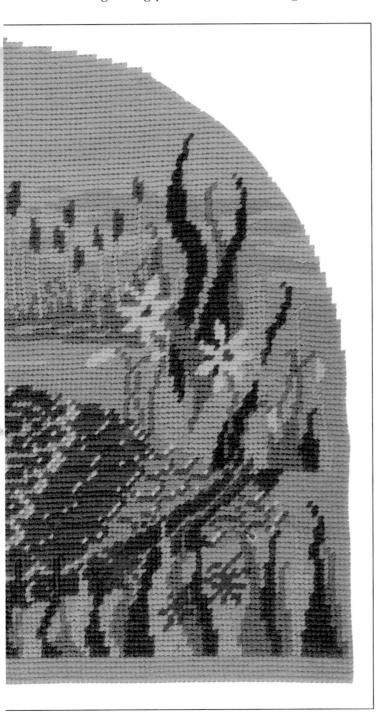

MATERIALS
Finished size 13 × 10½in (33 × 27cm)
Piece of 12-hole interlock canvas, size 17 × 14in (43 × 36cm)
Anchor Tapisserie wools:
One skein each of 9672 mist, 9774 cloud, 9794 grey, 8490 magenta, 8114 daffodil, 9658 smoke, 8036 ivory, 8006 pearl
Two skeins each of 9100 spring, 8990 emerald, 9094 willow, 8682 steel
Three skeins of 8774 azure
Short length of 8238 flame
Two pieces of wadding 16 × 13in (40 × 33cm)
Four pieces of washable cotton lining 16 × 13in (40 × 33cm)
Extra canvas and wools or fabric for the backing
Piece of cord 39in (1m)

PREPARATION
1 Mark the middle of the canvas with horizontal and vertical lines of basting stitches.

WORKING THE EMBROIDERY
2 Following the key and the colour photograph and working from the middle, stitch the embroidery using half cross stitch throughout.

FINISHING
3 Dampen the finished embroidery and pin it to a covered board, face downwards, allowing it to dry naturally (see page 105).
4 Turn up the last three rows of blue at the bottom of the two pieces and catch down on the wrong side using slipstitch.
5 Join the front and back together by sewing along the curved edges, right sides facing. Trim the excess canvas back to within ½in (12mm) of the embroidery.
6 Turn right sides out.
7 Sew the embroidery cord around the curved edge, attaching the ends about 1in (2.5cm) inside the tea-cosy, leaving a loop at the top.
8 Cut two teacosy shapes from the wadding, about ¼in (6mm) smaller all round.
9 Cut four pieces of lining fabric to the same size as the embroidery and join two pieces by sewing around the curve, right sides facing. Repeat with the other two pieces.
10 Turn right sides out and sew these two pieces together around the curve.
11 Insert the padding into the two sides and close the bottom edges of each side using slipstitch.
12 Place the padded lining inside the tea-cosy.

POND LIFE

Ponds are small, shallow bodies of water in which there is little difference in temperature between the surface and the bottom. No two ponds are alike as they vary in the amount of rich nutrients they contain which dictates the numbers and variety of animals and plants they can support.

Natural ponds are formed in various ways. They may be hollows resulting from glaciation, ox-bows cut off from rivers in flat, level valleys, streams blocked by landslides, pools formed behind barrier dunes, depressions left when a soluble rock such as limestone dissolves away and, in countries where the beaver constructs its dams there are, of course, beaver ponds. Man-made ponds, which used to epitomise the British village and originally made for watering animals, are now used to supply water for fire fighting, for raising fish, or as a by-product of the mining, gravel or clay industries. Garden ponds, which were originally built as ornaments, are just as capable of supporting a variety of animals and plants.

The most important factor for all ponds, naturally, is water. This is known as the 'universal solvent' because it will dissolve more substances than any other liquid. Carbon dioxide, oxygen and nitrogen are all essential to life and are absorbed into water from the atmosphere and through photosynthesis. Photosynthesis occurs when the plant's green pigment, chlorophyll, traps the energy of the sun and uses it to convert the simple inorganic compounds, carbon dioxide and water into complex organic substances, the sugars, which are the building blocks of life. During the synthesis oxygen is released which can sometimes be seen as constant streams of bubbles in the water. If the pond becomes full of dead organic matter decomposing by fungi and bacteria action, the level of oxygen will decrease and creatures will not survive, gradually leading to the death of the pond.

One of the most familiar aquatic plants is the water-lily with its showy flowers and large round

The emperor dragonfly (Anax imperator), although not threatened at present, could become extinct if ponds decrease in numbers or become polluted, which appears to be the current trend.

leaves which spread out over the water. The plants are supported by the water and therefore do not need as rigid a stem as those of land plants. The stems are soft and filled with spongy, air-filled tissue which keeps them boyant, so holding the leaves on the surface of the water. The flexible stems rise and fall in response to the changes in water level. The leaves of the water-lily are tough and leathery and can resist being battered and torn by wave action and heavy rain storms.

The flowers of the white water-lily (*Nymphae alba*) can grow up to 5in (12cm) across and are the largest of any wild flowers in the British Isles. The flowers open by midday and give off a fruity scent which attracts pollinating insects. Towards dusk the flowers fold shut and sink slightly into the water. These water-lilies, which are found Europe, Asia, north Africa and north-west America, have lost 90 per cent of their habitats since the 1930s due to water sports, pollution and drainage, as well as to unscrupulous collectors.

The emperor dragonfly (*Anax imperator*) is the largest of the dragonflies. It is a powerful predator and capable of very fast flight, feeding on other insects which it catches and often consumes in flight. Its eggs are anchored into incisions made in water plants such as broad-leaved pondweed, and hatch into aquatic predatory nymphs which live among the water-weed. Sluggish by habit, the nymph lurks in wait for its prey, capturing it with a swift movement of the hinged, strongly clawed mask. A well-grown nymph will take insects, tadpoles and small fish. After two or more years, the nymph crawls out of the water for the final moult or shedding of skin. The larval skin splits down the back, freeing the fully developed insect.

Today many ponds are in danger. Farmers no longer need them and so they are being neglected, drying up or being poisoned by weed-killers or fertilizers. Naturalists and conservationists are now trying to protect ponds, even building new ones, so pond life survives.

8006 pearl	8016 buttercup	9018 leaf
9560 copper	9006 green	8992 grass
	9800 black	
2 white cotton	290 yellow cotton	188 green cotton
143 blue cotton	112 purple cotton	403 black cotton

Like butterflies, dragonflies darting through the air are reminders of the countryside, hot summer days, picnics and cool, shady pools and streams. Their beautiful iridescent colours flash bright blue as they hover over a water-lily, tirelessly defending their territory and only settling to devour a particularly large prey or to wait for the sun to reappear. I have a pond in my garden where up to half a dozen of these incredible insects can be found during summer, their wings beating so fast that they drown the air with their noisy hum.

In this bellpull design I have used a simple water-lily and leaf design and then repeated it by reversing it. The dragonflies have all been stitched in petit point using stranded cotton, which gives them an iridescent shine. The brass fittings are easily available and the addition of a tassel at the bottom finishes off the bellpull handsomely. To make further use of this design, you might abstract a single water-lily motif for a diary cover, or use a dragonfly for the front of a needlecase, adding beads for glitter.

WATER-LILY AND DRAGONFLY BELLPULL

MATERIALS
Finished size 5¼ × 33in (13 × 84cm)
Piece of 10-hole double thread canvas 9 × 38in
  (23 × 97cm)
Anchor Tapisserie wools:
One skein each of 8992 grass, 9560 copper,
  8016 buttercup, 9018 leaf
Three skeins of 8006 pearl
Four skeins of 9006 green
Ten skeins of 9800 black
Anchor stranded cotton:
One skein each of 143 blue, 112 purple, 188 green,
  290 yellow, 403 black
Two skeins of 2 white
Lining fabric 7 × 36in (18 × 91cm)
Brass fittings
Tassel if required

PREPARATION
1 Mark the middle of the canvas with horizontal and vertical lines of basting stitches.

WORKING THE EMBROIDERY
2 Working from the key and the colour photograph, stitch the water-lilies, leaves, stems and background in the wool yarn using half cross stitch throughout.
3 Next, work the dragonflies using the stranded cotton, again in half cross stitch but working over single threads of canvas to create smaller stitches and a finer piece of work.

FINISHING
4 Dampen the finished embroidery and then pin it to a covered board and leaving it to dry naturally (see page 105).
5 With right sides together, stitch the backing fabric to the embroidery leaving a gap along one of the sides and a small gap at each corner to allow access for the brass bell pull fittings.
6 Trim the excess material to within ½in (12mm) of the embroidery, cutting the corners diagonally.
7 Turn right sides out and close the gap with slipstitch.
8 Fix the brass fittings to the top and bottom of the bellpull. A tassel can be sewn on to the bottom if required. Sew up the gaps.

THE SEA TURTLES

The turtle has a long evolutionary history as a water dwelling reptile going back about 90 million years. Like all reptiles, sea turtles first evolved on the land but developed to become aquatic creatures. Their limbs evolved into paddles and developed salt-excreting glands around the eyes. They are related to the tortoise, which is a land reptile, the fresh water turtle and also the amphibious terrapin.

Marine turtles spend most of their lives in the water but begin life on shore as hatchlings. After mating at sea the females swim inshore, usually at night, climb on to the beach and excavate a hole in the sand with their flippers. After laying around 100 eggs they cover them with sand and return to the sea. The hatchlings emerge about two months later and make their way towards the sea.

Both the eggs and babies are easy meals for many creatures. Dogs and coatis probe into the nest, ghost crabs burrow down to get the eggs and, when the eggs hatch, there are birds and fish waiting to catch them. Therefore, for even one or two baby turtles to survive, a great number of eggs must be laid. The body of a female turtle can only hold so many fully formed eggs and to ensure survival of the species, a female turtle returns to nest several times within a season, coming ashore at intervals of 10–14 days.

With long flippers and streamlined shapes, sea turtles are beautifully adapted for sustained travel through water. Their bony armour is less restricting than that of freshwater turtles and tortoises, making them more buoyant and agile, but their limbs and head cannot be completely retracted within the shell and are therefore vulnerable to shark attack. On land they move slowly and, once turned over on to their backs, are seldom able to right themselves.

There are seven species of sea turtle: the green, the leatherback, loggerhead, hawksbill olive, Kemp's Ridley and flatbacks, with the leatherback being the largest. Each has its

Marine turtles spend most of their lives in water but start their life on shore as hatchlings. Many of the young turtles do not reach the sea but become an easy meal for predators such as birds, crabs and even fish.

own somewhat specialized strategy for survival but there are common themes running through the lives of all species of sea turtle, especially when they come on land.

The major difference between the various species of turtle is in their diet which affects where they are to be found and their migration. The green turtles are herbivores living off turtle grass and algae, while other turtles are carnivores. Jellyfish are the main item in the diet of the leatherbacks, loggerhead turtles eat snails, mussels, crabs and other hard-shelled marine animals, hawksbills graze off sponges encrusting rocky areas while olive and Kemp's Ridleys eat shrimp, jellyfish, crabs and some algae. The flatbacks feed on seaweed and cuttlefish.

The green turtle is the best known species since its flesh is most highly regarded and in certain areas of the world the species has been grossly over-exploited for several hundreds years. Like the giant tortoise of the Galapagos Islands, the turtle provided fresh meat for sailors and was much sought after by the early navigators.

The most endangered turtle is Kemp's Ridley which is found in the Gulf of Mexico and in the Atlantic coastal waters of the southern USA. In the late 1940s over 42 000 nesting females were recorded in a single day. Now there are thought to be no more than 900 adult females remaining. The species is extremely vulnerable because its entire breeding range appears to be restricted to a section of coast at Rancho Nuevo in the State of Tamaulipas, Mexico.

WWF has a number of turtle projects worldwide. It is involved in action to prevent the illegal but still significant trade in tortoiseshell products for the luxury market, as well as education campaigns to control over-harvesting of turtles for food. In Greece and Turkey, WWF is aiming to save the turtle-nesting beaches from hotel developments and in Spain, is investigating the problem of turtles being caught in fishing nets.

TURTLE PINCUSHION

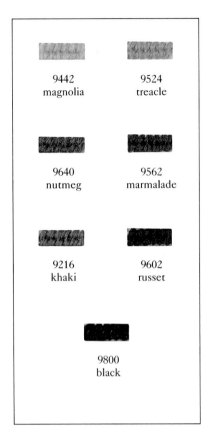

9442
magnolia

9524
treacle

9640
nutmeg

9562
marmalade

9216
khaki

9602
russet

9800
black

For a long time I wondered how to create a turtle design in needlepoint as the creatures are an odd shape and can come out looking like anything but a turtle! I decided on a very simple design, concentrating on the shapes found on the shell with the legs and head just stitched geometrically in two colours. Because of the detail on the turtle I felt it was best to leave the background plain. The little fish on the reverse of the pincushion is just a fun shape to do!

This design would come out larger if a coarser canvas was used. A 10-hole double thread canvas would increase the size by 1in (2.5cm) or 7-hole would make the design 7in (18cm) square. If using this very large canvas, double the yarn in the needle as a single strand will not cover the canvas. However, if you want to use the design to make a picture or cushion, the easiest way is to repeat the design several times on one piece of canvas of the size you require. Stitching nine of the turtles in a square with a border incorporating the little fish would look really charming. It is not necessary to keep to the colours I have used here – you can select a range to tone with your furnishings – or choose bright reds, oranges or blues to make a brilliant 'pop art' design.

MATERIALS
Finished size 4 × 4in (10 × 10cm)
Two pieces of 12-hole interlock canvas 6 × 6in (15 × 15cm)
Anchor Tapisserie wools:
One skein of 9562 marmalade
Three skeins of 9524 treacle
Small lengths of 9442 magnolia, 9602 russet, 9800 black, 9216 khaki, 9640 nutmeg
Toy stuffing

PREPARATION
1 Mark the middle of both pieces of canvas with horizontal and vertical lines of basting stitches.

WORKING THE EMBROIDERY
2 Stitch the front and back of the pincushions using half cross stitch throughout, following the key and the colour photograph.

FINISHING
3 Press the embroidery with a hot steam iron, gently pulling back into shape (see page 105).
4 Trim the unworked canvas to within ½in (12mm) of the embroidery, cutting into the corners diagonally.

5 Fold the unworked canvas to the wrong side of the embroidery.
6 Join the front and back of the pincushion together using long armed cross stitch (or over stitch), starting near the corner of one side and continuing round leaving a gap of 1in (2.5cm).
7 Fill the pin cushion with the toy stuffing, ensuring it gets into all the corners.
8 Close the gap by continuing the long armed cross stitch or over stitch.

Hatchlings that survive the shore predators and reach the sea, search for floating seaweed and may spend their first year sheltering under it.

STITCHING TECHNIQUES

Out of all the many endangered species in the world today I have chosen these few that are characteristic of four different habitats and have tried to incorporate elements of these habitats in the design. The elephant wallhanging, for example, shows a typical African landscape, with the little weaver birds' nest hanging from the acacia trees; the red-throated diver sits among reeds and bullrushes and the bears' picture has a border of luscious fruit. The designs vary from the simple to the advanced. The whales and dolphins are very simple shapes but by putting them with a rich background of turquoise and blue, mixing these two colours in such a way to give masses of movement, actually enhances the simplicity of the mammals.

I have tried to make all the designs in this book as realistic as possible using wools and silks to get the required effects of fur, feathers or iridescent wing-tips. For the animals that have lots of fur, such as the tiger and lion, I have used subtle shading effects to make them more lifelike, incorporating single stitches of colour haphazardardly worked in amongst the larger blocks. Without this, the designs might look very flat and dull, lacking the movement they have here. I designed the birds, such as the owl and parrots, in a slightly different manner, making their features more stylized which, interestingly, still makes them appear lifelike. Again, by adding little dots of colour within each feather, they acquire texture and do not appear 'flat' and are exciting to look at time and time again.

CHOOSING YARNS
For all the designs I have used Anchor tapisserie yarn which is easily available from most needlework or haberdashery shops.

Unlike knitting yarn the Anchor tappieserie yarn does not vary from dye lot to dye lot. This means you can buy the yarn in small quantities until the work is finished. I found it great fun to pick and choose colours for the designs, keeping the shades as close as possible to the subject and ensuring the backgrounds were in keeping. In some of the designs I have also used Anchor stranded cottons which are ideal for adding lustre to elements of the design. The dragonflies in the bellpull, for instance, have been stitched using six

different colours in tiny stitches to make them as delicate as possible, capturing their brilliance. The butterfly pincushions and stool cover have had stranded cotton stitched over the tapisserie wool to add shine. For all designs I used a size 20 tapestry needle which is perfect for all gauges of canvas and can be used with both the wool and the stranded cottons.

Always remember that you will have to adjust the wool quantities shown here if you change the canvas.

CARING FOR YOUR DESIGNS
All the embroideries in this book are 100 per cent pure wool and therefore can easily be cleaned. If a cushion needs cleaning, it can be done at a dry cleaners if the cushion pad is taken out. For footstools, and the smaller items such as pincushions and spectacle cases, a good spot upholstery cleaner will get rid of dirt. If coffee or ink is spilt on the work it is important to rinse it under running cold water immediately, leave it to dry naturally and then press it. If the strain still shows it may be wise to unpick the area and then restitch it.

If after several years of wear the embroidery appears to be wearing thin, it is best to unpick the area and restitch it. It is a good idea to store a few strands of each of the yarn colours used in a project, just in case restitching has to bee done in later years.

When unstitching, carefully tuck the needle under the particular stitch on the front of the embroidery, pull slightly and snip using a very sharp pair of small scissors. The stitches on either side can then be pulled through. If at any time the yarn appears to be caught, never tug at it, just slip the needle through the caught stitch and snip it again.

WORKING THE DESIGNS
Before starting any of these designs it is important to mark the centre of the canvas with basting stitches. These are running stitches which run horizontally and vertically across the canvas and divide the canvas into four quarters. This makes it easier to follow the colour picture and ensures that your embroidery is centred on the canvas.

Having cut the yarn to 15in (38cm) lengths and

threaded your needle, start by passing the needle down through the canvas about 1in (2.5cm) from where the first stitch is to be made. Leave an end about 4in (10cm) long on the right side of the canvas. Bring the needle through for the first stitch. Finish off the starting end later by taking it through to the back and finishing as shown on page 105.

Always work in good light and try to keep the tension of the threads the same throughout. The canvas can be put into a frame to keep it taut (available from most needlework shops) or worked without a frame. If the canvas begins to catch your clothing, cover the edges with masking tape.

It is important to keep an even tension over the whole of the work which gives a professional finish. This either comes naturally right away or it may take you a while to get the hang of it. Practise several rows of stitches on small pieces of canvas and try to keep the tension the same all the way through. Also, try ending a thread and joining a new thread in the middle of a row as this is a test to see if your tension remains the same when beginning to stitch again. But do not worry

if the embroidery does look uneven as a good pressing on the wrong side with a hot steam iron will tend to flatten out imperfections.

The majority of the designs have been stitched using a half cross stitch but in some I have used cross stitch and knots. The cross stitch is used where a particular colour needs to stand out, such as the whiskers on the tiger cushion, and the knots are an effective method of making flowers, as on the rhino footstool. Other stitches can be used to give an alternative effect but if you do decide to change the stitches, remember that the wool quantities given will have to be altered.

I have mentioned 'petit point' in the water-lily and dragonfly bellpull design. Gross point is needlepoint stitched on double thread canvas, while petite point is stitched on single thread canvas. The effect of each can be very similar or totally different depending on the gauge of canvas. In the bellpull design you can see that the dragonflies are very finely stitched using all the holes in the 10-hole canvas which is equal to 20 holes per 1in (2.5cm). The rest of the design is worked over the double threads, thus 10 holes per 1in (2.5cm).

The tiger's whiskers on this cushion design (pages 14–15) were made to stand out from the embroidery by working them in cross stitch, using white wool.

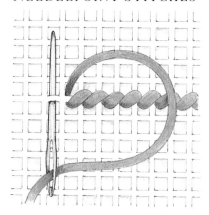

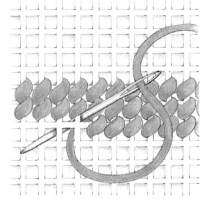

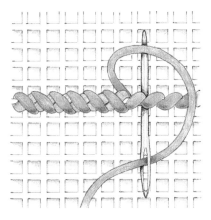

Half cross stitch

This stitch can be worked from right to left, or left to right as you prefer. It is important that all the stitches slope in the same direction on the front with the back showing short vertical stitches. When ending a length of yarn, pass it through a few stitches at the back or merely catch it into the next row.

Tent stitch

This is a more hardwearing stitch as it completely covers the canvas as opposed to the half cross stitch which, in effect, only covers the face of the embroidery. However, it does use more yarn (sometimes up to a third more) which should be noted when buying materials for any particular design.

Cross stitch

This stitch forms a cross on the front of the design. Work a row of half cross stitches and then work back in the opposite direction. When mixing half cross and cross stitches in one design I make the top cross stitch run in the opposite direction to the rest of the half cross stitches for maximum effect.

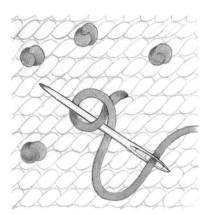

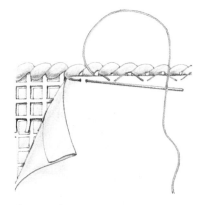

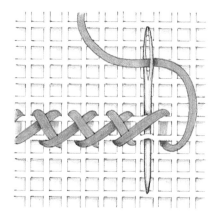

Knots

Once you have practised this to get the right tension in the knot, you will find these stitches very easy to do. Bring the yarn to the front of the canvas in the required position, hold it down with your thumb, encircle it with the needle and pull through. Insert the needle back through the canvas behind the knot.

Slipstitch

This is a neat way to join embroidery to lining fabric when making up spectacle cases or purses. It is very quick and simple to do and ensures no unworked canvas is shown. Slipstitching is also used to close open seams and is almost invisible when worked correctly.

Long armed cross stitch

I have used this decorative stitch to join the fronts and backs of pincushions. It is similar to cross stitch but the 'crosses' are worked closer together and with a longer top stitch, leaving no canvas showing. It looks rather like a mixture of a herringbone and cross stitch.

CHOOSING YOUR CANVAS

By choosing canvases of different mesh the designs can be altered. If one particular design uses 10-hole canvas and you would prefer the result to be smaller, then use a 12-hole or 14-hole canvas. Alternatively, if you want to enlarge the design, use a coarser canvas remembering that a doubled yarn may be needed to cover the canvas.

Many of the designs in this book could be worked on rug canvas, using rug wool, working either in cross or half cross stitch.

When stitching be careful that the yarn does not fray as this will show in the finished embroidery as a thin thread. The best way to ensure against this is to only use lengths of 15in (38cm) long. The longer the yarn is the more often it rubs through the canvas and this causes fraying.

FINISHING OFF THE DESIGN

When the embroidery has been completed the canvas may be slightly askew. This is easily rectified by dampening it on the back with warm water, pinning it firmly to a board covered with a tea towel or piece of blotting paper and allowing it to dry naturally. Press it quickly with a hot steam iron, again on the back, and the design should be ready to make up.

MARKING CANVAS

Some embroiderers like to mark designs or centre lines directly on to the canvas. If you do this, it is important that you use a waterproof pen. If non-waterproof markers are used, the colour can run when you dampen the embroidery for blocking and completely spoil your work

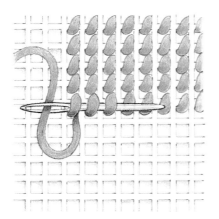

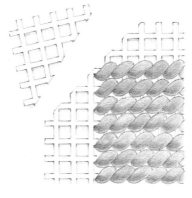

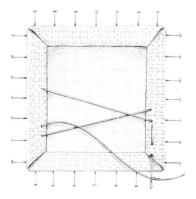

Starting and finishing

Many people tie a knot in the yarn end to start. I sometimes do myself – but it is not the best way to work. Start by passing the needle down through the canvas about 1in (2.5cm) from where the first stitch is to be. Leave a 4in (10cm) end. Work the stitches. Finish by taking the yarn end to the wrong side. Pass the needle through the backs of the worked stitches. Finish the starting end in the same way.

Cutting corners

After finishing the stitching of a cushion or a pincushion, or a piece which is to be lined, the corners of the canvas are cut diagonally. This avoids a bulk of canvas at the corners after making up which could distort the finished work.

Lacing for framing

Many of these designs can be turned into pictures by mounting them on a board and framing them. When the embroidery is finished and is straight cut a piece of board about ¼inch (6mm) thick to a size just slightly smaller than the finished needlepoint. Secure the embroidery to the board with pins pushed into the edges, stretching it smoothly and tightly as you work. Then lace the unworked pieces of canvas together, first horizontally then vertically, starting in the centre and working towards the corners.

MOUNTING STOOL TOPS

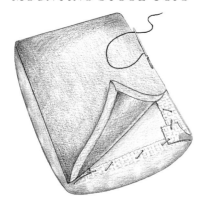

Most stools are sold with removable, ready-made pads. Lift out the pad and spread the finished, trimmed embroidery on the top. Centre it and then pin in place temporarily. Turn the pad over and insert pins into the middle of the four sides of the pad, securing the canvas. Stretch the canvas, working on all four sides, pinning and repinning as you work until the canvas is smooth on the pad and fairly taut. You can either staple the canvas to the wood border or lace the edges of the canvas together as shown on page 105. Remove all pins. Finish by sewing a fabric backing to the underside of the pad. Round stool canvases should be laced rather than stapled.

The wolves footstool embroidery (pages 58–59) is for a stool 14in (35cm) square. The design could be enlarged for a bigger stool or a chair seat by extending the background.

HOW TO USE THIS BOOK

Each of the designs has been photographed both as a made-up item and then flat, so that every stitch can be seen. You work the designs from the flat photographs. First, measure and mark the centre points on the sides, then pencil in horizontal and vertical lines, to mark the middle of the design. (Pencil can be erased from the page later without spoiling your book.) Put the canvas into a frame, if you are using one, or cover the cut edges with masking tape.

Measure and mark the middle of your canvas with horizontal and vertical lines of basting threads (or use a waterproof embroidery pen). You are now ready to begin stitching.

Working from the colour picture and matching your wool colours to the key, work the design from the middle outwards in half cross stitch. Working from the middle has two advantages: one, your embroidery will be exactly centred on the canvas and, two, there is less risk of your distorting the canvas if you are working without a frame.

As you stitch, try not to take threads across the back of the canvas from one area to another. This practice will, inevitably, make your work thick and bulky on the back. It is far better to finish the wool end by working it under the back of 2 or 3 stitches. Clip the piece off and keep it by you for when you need to work just a few stitches in that particular colour.

WORKING FROM CHARTS
Although it is not difficult to stitch from a picture some people prefer to work from symbol charts. I have prepared a chart for each of the designs in this book and they are available by post from the address on page 112.

When working from symbols charts, I suggest you copy the symbols and mark them alongside the colour keys. In this way, you will not find yourself using the wrong colour.

IDEAS FOR THE PATTERNS
Most of the designs in this book are all within the expertise of the average embroiderer and some of the patterns are small, and simple enough for children to do. The Panda pincushion and needlecase on page 32 for instance, and the butterfly and turtle pincushions on pages 74 and 100, are ideal

designs for children. Any of these designs could also be worked in cross stitch on coarser Binca fabric, to make pictures.

Needlework greetings cards make very acceptable gifts or fund-raising items and the smaller designs are ideal for this purpose. You could try working them on a finer canvas mesh, perhaps a 14-hole or even 18-hole and this will reduce finished size of the embroidery.

USING THE DESIGNS
Although I have designed the embroideries for a specific use – cushions, stool tops, pictures or firescreens etc, there is no reason why you should not use the designs for other furnishings or accessories. The square cushion designs, for instance, can be enlarged to make rectangular-shaped cushions by working extra background at top and bottom. Or you can make bigger cushions by working three or four bands of solid colour inside the decorative borders.

The cushion designs are also ideal for working chair seats. As these are often wider at the front of the seat and narrower at the back, work the main design in the middle of your canvas and then work the background to the desired shape, omitting the border.

The large, animal head designs would make very impressive embroideries for magazine covers or stationery folders. Experiment by working on double-thread canvas. Work the animal head stitches between the threads so that you reduce the scale of the design, then work the background stitches across the double threads.

The borders on the cushions provide you with a wealth of designs which you can adapt and use for decorative furnishings, such as curtain tie backs or bellpulls. Or you might try repeating a border across the canvas 5 or 6 times, the edges touching, to make a smart and modern-looking cushion. Small areas of the borders can be adapted for spectacles and sunglasses cases or for small pincushions and bookmarks.

For a really large project, and to remind you of the important work of the WWF, why not adapt six different animal designs for a wallhanging or rug. Work each of the designs as square shapes with 3 or 4 rows of stitches in a solid colour between the designs to link them.

INDEX

WWF OFFICES

WWF International
Avenue du Mont-Blanc
CH–1196 Gland

**WWF Affiliate National
Organisations**

WWF Australia
Level 10, 8–12 Bridge Street
GPO Box 528
Sydney NSW 2001

WWF Austria
Ottakringerstr. 114–116/9
Postfach 1
A–1162 Vienna

WWF Belgium
608 Chaussée de Waterloo
B–1060 Brussels

WWF Canada
90 Eglinton Ave. E
Suite 504
Toronto
Ontario M4P 2Z7

WWF Denmark
Ryesgade 3 F
DK–2200 Copenhagen N

WWF Finnland
Uudenmaankatu 40
SF–00120 Helsinki 12

WWF France
151 Blvd. de la Reine
F–78000 Versailles

WWF Germany
Hedderichstr. 110
P.O. Box 70 11 27
D–6000 Frankfurt a/M 70

*Elephant herds can number up to 40
family members. Males stay with the herd
until they are about 12 years old. Then
leave the group, sometimes to live alone.*

WWF Hong Kong
No. 1, Tramway Path
GPO Box 12721
Hong Kong

WWF India
P.O. Box 3058
127B Lodi Road
New Delhi 110 003

WWF Italy
Via Salaria 290/221
I–00199 Rome

WWF Japan
Nihonseimei Akabanebashi
Bldg. 7F, 3–1–14 Shiba
Minato-ku
Tokyo 105

WWF Malaysia
3rd Floor Wisma IJM Annexe
Jalan Yong Shook Lin
Locked bag No 911
46990 Petaling Jaya

WWF Netherlands
Postbus 7
NL–3700 AA Zeist

WWF New Zealand
35, Taranaki Street, 2.F
P.O. Box 6237
Wellington

WWF Norway
Kristian Augustsgt 7A
PB 6784 St Olavspl
0130 Oslo

WWF Pakistan
P.O. Box 5180
Model Town
54600 Lahore

WWF South Africa
P.O. Box 456
Stellenbosch 7600

WWF Spain
ADENA
Santa Engracia
E-Madrid 28010

WWF Sweden
Ulriksdals Slott
S–171 71 Solna

WWF Switzerland
Förrlibuckstr. 66
Postfach
CH–8037 Zürich

WWF United Kingdom
Panda House
Weyside Park
Godalming
Surrey GU7 1XR

WWF United States
1250 24th St. N.W.
Washington D.C. 20037

**WWF Associate
National Organisations**

Fundacion vida Silvestre
Argentina
DEFENSA 245 51, 6 Piso
1065 Capital Federal
Buenos Aires, Argentina

Fundacion Natura
Av. América 5653
y Voz Andes
Casilla 253
Quito, Ecuador

Nigerian Conservation
Foundation
P.O. Box 74683
Victoria Island
Lagos, Nigeria

Wildlife Fund Thailand
251/88–90 Phaholyothin Road
Bangkhan
Bangkok 10220, Thailand

Fudena
Avenida Principal Los
Cortijos de Lourdes C/2A
P.O. Box 70376
Caracas 1071–A, Venezuela

ACKNOWLEDGEMENTS

My warmest thanks should firstly go to my husband Andrew whose constant encouragement and generous support has helped me enormously while writing this book. I would also like to specially thank my parents, and other members of my family and my friends who have all been very helpful and patient.

Thank you also to Jo Mee, Eden Thomson and Andrea Ballard at the World Wide Fund for Nature in Godalming, Surrey. They have been of tremendous help with the research, providing up-to-date facts for all the animals and plants in this book.

I would also like to give my thanks to Susan Rockley, Alison McClymont and Louise McDermott who helped me enormously by stitching some of the embroideries quickly and superbly and special thanks to Lucinda Symons for her imaginative photography which has brought these designs to life.

The publishers would like to thank the following companies and organisations for their help in producing this book:

Erica Vandersteen for properties search; Global Village, London SW3 for Safari furniture and accessories; Cynthia and Ken Prior, Norah and Geoffrey Godbar, Christopher Baker, Lucy Wiggins and Far Horizons Gallery, Petersfield, Hampshire for accessories; Shopwyke Garden Centre, Chichester, Hampshire and Highgate Garden Centre, London for plants; Coats Patons Crafts, PO Box, McMullen Road, Darlington, Co Durham, DL1 1YQ for yarns and threads; Harland Ltd, Rye, East Sussex for footstools.

Many of the designs in this book are available as kits from: Casa Needlepoint, 39 Merton Avenue, London W4 1TA. Please send a stamped addressed envelope for a price list.

Charts for the designs are also available. Send a stamped addressed envelope to the same address.

Casa Needlepoint kits may be obtained in Australia from:

Kim Lauren Exclusives, 53 William Edward Street, Longueville, New South Wales, 2066.

PICTURE CREDITS

The photographs on the following pages are reproduced with the permission of: *p6* WWF (Olwyn Standbrook): *p10* WWF (Storm Stanley): *p12* WWF (D. Lawson): *p16* WWF (Bill Wilson): *p20* WWF (T. Brzozowski)): *p24* WWF (Mike Corley): *p29* WWF (P.E. Parker): *p30* WWF (Olwyn Standbrook): *p34* WWF (Ian Exton): *p38* NHPA (J. Carmichael): *p42* Bruce Coleman Ltd: *p46, 49* WWF (Rod Williams): *p50* WWF (N. Atherton): *p52* Bruce Coleman Ltd (Legrand): *p56* WWF (P.J. Banks): *p60* Bruce Coleman Ltd (A.J. Dean): *p64* Bruce Coleman Ltd (Ernest Duscher): *p68* WWF (D. Murrell): *p72* WWF (Brian Massey): *p76* WWF (J. Jackson): *p78* WWF (F. Jackson): *p82* WWF (Nicky White): *p86* WWF (Duncan Murrell): *p89* WWF (Paul Coppi): *p90* Bruce Coleman Ltd (Gordon Langsbury): *p92* Bruce Coleman Ltd (Jan Van de Kam): *p94* Bruce Coleman Ltd (Geoff Doré): *p98* WWF (Urs Woy): *p101* WWF (M. Rautkari): *p110* WWF